First published in 2004 by New Holland Publishers (UK) Ltd
London • Cape Town • Sydney • Auckland
Garfield House, 86–88 Edgware Road, London W2 2EA, United Kingdom
www.newhollandpublishers.com
80 McKenzie Street, Cape Town 8001, South Africa
Level 1, Unit 4, 14 Aquatic Drive, Frenchs Forest, NSW 2086, Australia
218 Lake Road, Northcote, Auckland, New Zealand

ISBN 1 84330 676 X
10 9 8 7 6 5 4 3 2 1

Editorial Direction: Rosemary Wilkinson Senior Editor: Clare Hubbard Production: Hazel Kirkman

Designed and created for New Holland by AG&G Books Copyright © 2004 "Specialist" AG&G Books
Design: Glyn Bridgewater Illustration: Gill Bridgewater Editor: Fiona Corbridge
Photographs: AG&G Books, Ian Parsons, John Freeman, OASE and Forsham Cottage Arks

Reproduction by Pica Digital Pte Ltd, Singapore

Printed and bound in Malaysia by Times Offset (M) Sdn. Bhd.

The essential guide to designing, building, improving, and maintaining ponds and water features

A. & G. Bridgewater

Contents

Authors' foreword

Water is our most precious resource and one of our most tantalizing natural elements. Water has irresistible magical qualities that give us pleasure—we may be inspired by the beautiful sight and sound of a romantic fountain, or feel stress evaporate as we sit alongside a bubbling stream. Artists and poets are stimulated into creativity by mysterious lakes, crashing seas, and sparkling crystal springs, and children delight in splashing around in puddles and paddling pools.

At one time, only the wealthy could consider building a pond or water feature, because it was an expensive business to move soil, line ponds with clay, and set up steam pumps to move water around. Today, however, new technology has brought the whole area of using water for pleasure and decoration within the scope of the ordinary gardener. With the introduction of flexible liners, PVC piping, and small, low-voltage electric pumps everything is possible.

So if you fantasize about adding a water feature to your plot, whether it's a small pond in a container, a fountain, or maybe a large pond to attract wildlife, now is the time to realize your dreams. This book will guide you through all the stages of choosing a project, from selecting tools and materials to design and construction, and stocking with plants and animals. At the end of it all, you will have a uniquely beautiful water feature for the whole family to enjoy.

Measurements

This book uses metric measurements. To convert these to imperial measurements, multiply the figure given in the text by the relevant number shown in the table below. Conversions are approximate.

To convert	Multiply by
inches to millimeters	25.4
feet to meters	0.3048
yards to meters	0.9144
sq. inches to sq. millimeters	645.16
sq. feet to sq. meters	0.092903
sq. yards to sq. meters	0.83612
cu. feet to cu. meters	0.02831
cu yards to cu. meters	0.7646
pounds to grams	453.592
pounds to kilograms	0.4536
gallons to litres	4.545

Assessing your garden

Whether you have a small yard in a city or a more spacious garden in the country, there is a pond or water feature to suit the situation. The secret of success with a project is to make sure that there is a balance between the size and character of your garden and that of the pond or water feature. Spend time in your garden carefully choosing the site and planning the operation, then work out how best to source the materials.

Will there be enough room in my garden?

GARDEN SIZE

Walk around your garden. Is the space big enough for a pond? Or would it be better if you had a small water feature? If your garden is very small, such as a walled courtyard, it may be more fitting to have a small feature with lots of movement and sound, rather than to fill most of the space with an ornamental pond. Also, consider how the project is going to affect the way other members of the household use the garden.

→ *Sometimes less is more! A small water feature can transform a dull inner-city courtyard into a pleasant place to sit and relax.*

OTHER ASPECTS

When you have weighed up the size of your garden against the style of the item that you would like to build, you need to consider the implications of going ahead with the project.

You may have decided that the garden is big enough for a medium-size pond, but this project involves a lot of digging and will produce a heap of excavated soil. Have you considered where you are going to put it? Are you going to have the soil removed or could it be recycled and used for a raised border or a rockery?

Think about the impact the proposed project will have on other people. If, for example, you have a tiny garden and are planning to have a small fountain set over a sump, will the noise be an irritation for your neighbors? If you have young children, have you chosen a project with their safety in mind?

GARDEN STYLE

↑ *A carefully considered formal pond, such as this canal, can turn an otherwise boring patio into a magical place where it's a pleasure to while away the hours.*

There are two basic styles of pond and water feature: informal and formal (or you might say natural and architectural). However, the choice you make will to a great extent be dictated by the form and age of your house; the shape and size of your garden; and, of course, your own particular likes and dislikes.

The proposed site for the project must also be given some careful thought. If you would prefer a natural, informal pond, it doesn't make much sense to position it on a courtyard patio. Similarly, a formal raised pond, complete with a fountain, would look out of place in a wooded glade.

Study your garden and decide how much time you want to spend on construction now and maintenance in the future; think about the possible materials (stone, brick, concrete, or wood) and then choose a style that will look good in the existing surroundings.

↑ *Enjoy the tranquility of a Japanese garden by transforming an ordinary pond with the addition of rocks, low-growing shrubs, and a statue.*

Pond and water feature options

What will be best for my garden?

There are pond and water feature designs to suit every budget and transform your garden. Would you like a small wildlife pond complete with tadpoles, frogs, and newts? Or do you want a formal pond with goldfish and paved surrounds? Do you need a pond to complement a cottage garden, or is it going to be the focus of a city courtyard garden? Perhaps a trickling water feature for the patio is more your style. The following examples will give you some ideas.

TYPES OF POND

Raised formal pond

↗ A raised formal pond makes an eye-catching addition to any garden. It is low-maintenance, relatively quick and simple to build, and avoids the need to dig a hole. Fish and plants are easy to view and it is also a safer option if you have young children. (See page 28.)

Sunken formal pond
Geometrically shaped

↘ The formal, usually circular, hole-in-the-ground pond is a popular choice. This type of pond means digging a hole and moving large quantities of soil, but the introduction of preformed and flexible liners has done away with the need to mix concrete to line the pond. (See pages 24–27, 37.)

Wildlife pond
Irregular in shape; an informal pond

↘ If you want to create an irregularly shaped hole-in-the-ground pond, to look like a country pond that is a haven for frogs, toads, insects, and aquatic plants, the wildlife pond is an exciting possibility. This type of pond will very quickly become a back-to-nature playground for the whole family to enjoy. (See page 32.)

Fish and plants

Fish ~ You can either introduce fish, or you can let native wildlife take over and wait for frogs, newts, and suchlike to appear. You cannot easily have both. (See pages 44–45.)

Plants ~ When planting a pond, the object is to achieve a "balance" between the amounts of oxygen and algae in the water to ensure clear, sweet water. (See pages 38–43.)

POND LINERS

Liners ensure that a pond holds water. You can use a preformed plastic or resin liner, a flexible liner, or lay concrete. (See pages 24–27.)

Preformed liner ~ preformed liners look tempting in their simplicity, but they are expensive, small, and surprisingly tricky to fit. Resin ones last longer than those made of polypropylene.

Flexible liners ~ If you want to build a pond of your own design—to any size you like—a flexible liner is the best choice. Top-quality pond-grade butyl rubber liner will last a lifetime.

Concrete liner ~ If you enjoy hard work and want a long-lasting pond for the lowest possible cost, concrete is the answer.

POND ADDITIONS

Fountain

↗ A formal pond makes the perfect setting for a fountain. A fountain is powered by a pump—and nowadays small, low-voltage, submersible electric pumps are available, which are inexpensive to buy and easy to fit. (See pages 48–49, 68–69, 75.)

Cascade

↗ A cascade is a series of small waterfalls that trickle into each other, rather like water running down a flight of stairs. Choose a modern, sculptural effect or imitate nature with layers of rocks and boulders. (See pages 50–51.)

Waterfall

↗ A waterfall is a body of water falling off a shelf, but this effect can be achieved only if you have a steeply sloping site or a rocky outcrop. If not, you have to be prepared to import vast quantities of soil and rock to build the waterfall. (See pages 50–51.)

SMALL WATER FEATURES

Sculpture and automata

↗ If you enjoy mechanical movement, build this Japanese deer scarer, which uses trickling water to create a see-saw movement. (See page 72.)

Miniature pot fountain

↗ A diminutive fountain that produces a bubbling effect—a good option if you are worried about your children's safety. (See page 75.)

Wall mask waterspout

→ A wall or patio can be wonderfully enhanced by the addition of a mask concealing a waterspout. A mask is mounted on the wall and water is pumped up from a small reservoir through the mask to gush back into the reservoir. For a self-contained water feature, or to embellish an existing pond or plain wall, this is a good option. (See page 70.)

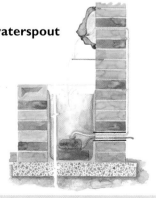

OTHER PONDS AND WATER FEATURES

There are many ways of adding interest to the garden with other water features, planting schemes, and structures.

Canal ~ Create an impressive body of moving water with the minimum of work and effort. A shallow trench is dug for the canal and water is pumped into it so that it overflows into a reservoir pool. The canal can either be built level with the ground or as a raised pond. (See pages 30–31.)

Container pond ~ Any size of container can be used, from a ceramic pot to a large water tank, as long as it is decorative and movable when empty. (See page 66.)

Bog garden ~ Though bog gardens can be built as features in their own right, they are best created as overflow areas at the side of an existing pond. They will enhance the overall shape of a pond and extend the area available for planting. (See pages 54–55.)

Bridge over a pond ~ Bridges are uniquely dynamic structures. If you have a good-size pond and the idea of building a bridge appeals, take the opportunity to enhance your garden with a striking structure in wood, stone, or brick. (See pages 58–59.)

Checking the site

Is there anything else to consider?

Before getting started, check the site to make sure that there aren't any factors that are going to cause difficulties. You need to take into account the position of underground drains, the slope and water table of the land, where the power supply will run from, existing trees, the way the sun affects the site at different times of day, and so on. Draw up a hit-list of potential problems, and make sure that they aren't going to hold you back.

THINGS TO CONSIDER WHEN SITING A POND OR WATER FEATURE

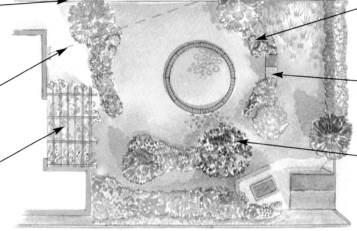

Windbreak
A tall fence provides shelter from the wind and will help to deaden the sound of traffic.

Service pipes
Make sure that the pond is sited well away from underground service pipes.

Viewpoint
Site the pond so that you can enjoy looking at it from the house or a patio.

Boggy ground
If the garden has areas of wet, soft ground, do not site the pond near these.

Seat
Position a seat near the pond so you can observe visiting wildlife.

Shade
A tree (not too near to the pond) can be used to supply dappled shade at the hottest time of day.

SITE CHECKLIST

Stand on the proposed site and slowly look around you. Look at the house, the trees, the position of the sun and neighboring houses. Try to take all the factors into account.

Sun and shade ~ Assess how the sun affects the site in the morning, afternoon, and evening. Avoid the extremes of heavy shade and full sun during the hottest part of the day. If it is feasible, the best situation is a site with full sun in the morning and evening, and dappled sunlight at noon.

Scale, orientation, and viewpoints ~ Walk around the garden in order to view the site from a good number of positions. Do you want to be able to see the pond or water feature from indoors? Do you want to be able to sit alongside it?

Providing shelter ~ It is no good siting a decorative pond on an exposed site. Most ponds need shelter for the plants to grow successfully; it also makes it a more pleasant place to visit. Is there an existing windbreak you can take advantage of?

Problems above and below ground ~ Avoid a site that is crisscrossed with underground service pipes and overhead cables. Avoid building a pond near plants with sharp roots, such as bamboo, which might pierce the pond liner. Likewise, keep away from tree roots, because they might cause concrete to crack.

Soil type and digging ~ Dig a test hole to check whether it is possible to build on that site. A rocky site is fine for a shallow pond, but is no good for a deep pond. A wet, clay soil is heavy to dig, but lets you dig a clean-sided hole without fear of subsidence. Avoid sites where there is a lot of movement of water about 12 inches below ground level, or where there are pockets of bad-smelling water.

PRESERVING PRECIOUS TOPSOIL

If you need to dig a deep hole for a pond, you will reach the sterile subsoil. Take care not to lose the fertile topsoil, which is the layer plants need to grow. As you strip away the topsoil, put it to one side. Shovel the subsoil onto an area that needs to be built up. Finally, bring the topsoil back to the site and spread it over the subsoil.

PROBLEMS UNDERGROUND

If the site for a pond is boggy, there is a risk that the water will deform a pond liner or even crack concrete. Although you can overcome the problem by laying underground drainage pipes or even fitting an underground sump complete with a pump, sometimes it is easier to opt for another location; alternatively, go for a raised pond that doesn't require digging into the soil.

Designing a project

A design needs to be more than a quick sketch on a scrap of paper. Once you have decided on the type, overall style, and location of the pond or water feature, it is vital to develop the idea on paper, noting all the measurements, facts, and figures. You will then be able to order your materials in the confident assurance that there won't be any horrible little surprises to catch you out. Extra thought at this stage will save you hours of aggravation and lots of cash!

What do I need to include in my design?

How to start

Get yourself a looseleaf folder complete with plain and gridded paper, pencils, a rule, and colored crayons. List your needs. If the design includes brick and stone, decide on colors and textures. Don't be too specific at this stage, just try to visualize the overall shape, color, and form.

YOUR CONCEPT

You may know that you want to build a raised pond rather than a wildlife pond, but are you aware of the available materials, their colors and textures? Look at as many books and magazines as possible. Talk over the idea with your family and friends.

VISUALIZING

Cover the ground with something the same size as the feature, such as sheets of plastic. Live with this full-size plan for a few days and see how it impacts on your use of the garden. Could it be bigger? Does it need to be realigned?

DESIGN CONSIDERATIONS

When designing a pond, look closely at the dimensions of your chosen materials (the pond-grade bútyl rubber or preformed liner, and the bricks and blocks) before working out the final size of the structure.

If, for example, you are building a raised pond, the starting point for the design will be the width, length, and height of the preformed liner. Without compromising the design, attempt to build the walls of the pond from a whole number of bricks to avoid having to cut them. Try to use all the materials to their full potential.

DRAWING YOUR DESIGN

Measure your garden and draw the plan to scale on gridded paper, so that each square is a set measurement. Draw the water feature on the plan so that its position is distanced from fixed points, such as the house and one of the boundary lines. If you are building a structure made from manufactured materials (bricks, slabs, or blocks), such as a raised pond, draw out the various views. As far as possible, size the structure so that it uses whole units in order to minimize complex cutting.

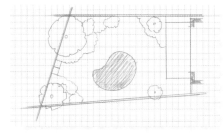

↗ *Draw the house on a horizontal or vertical axis of the grid, then plot existing features such as walls and trees. Draw movable items, such as the pond, on card. Cut out and try in various positions on the grid before finalizing.*

Checklist

• Is the design suited to your space? (Consider size and style.)

• Have you worked out the exact dimensions (and do they need to relate to material sizes)?

• Have you chosen the materials best suited to the design?

• Is the design structurally sound?

• Do you know how it is constructed?

• Have you incorporated the pipework?

FOOTINGS

If you are using brick, stone, or blocks, you will first need to build a stable footing under the structure. This will ensure that the structure resists summer and winter ground movement, and stays in one piece.

Designing with brick

Good brickwork means designing a structure that minimizes the need to cut bricks; also the vertical joints should be offset in neighboring courses. In most instances, manufactured items such as preformed pond liners and concrete slabs are compatible with whole brick sizes.

WHAT TO DO WITH PIPEWORK

Pipes are used to protect electric power cables and conduct water. Ideally, all pipes need to be buried. Water supply pipes are ribbed to resist crushing and kinking, and come in diameters ranging from $1/2$ inch through to $1^1/2$ inches. Be generous with pipe lengths.

When you have chosen a pump, check its inlet and outlet dimensions and buy the water supply pipe to fit. Protect the power cable with PVC conduit, reinforced PVC hosepipe, or ribbed water pipe. Set the pipes in a trench, then cover them with old bricks followed by plastic sheet and soil.

Planning and preparation

How do I prepare ahead?

Plan the whole project like a military operation. Now is the time for drawing up lists, working out quantities, scheduling when you are going to do the work, deciding whether or not you need help with the heavier tasks, and calling around for prices and delivery times. If you painstakingly plan out the small details—from where the materials are going to be stored to who is going to help on the day—the project will run like a dream!

SORTING OUT THE ORDER OF WORK

Each project needs to be planned out according to your particular situation, which is governed by the time of year, the size of your garden, who is helping, and so on. Your initial task is to decide on the order of work— what goes where, and when, and how.

Let's say that you are going to build a large, natural or wildlife pond with a flexible liner. You have got to dig a hole, and you will be using lots of bricks, sand, and cement. The basic order of work is to dig the hole, lay footings for the wall and top with concrete, rake sand into the hole, spread the liner, build a low wall, fill the pond with water, then landscape and plant. Decide ahead where all the excavated soil is going, and where you are going to put the bricks and cement. You don't want them spread out all over the place—you need a clear passage around the garden, and you don't want the materials getting damaged. It's important to plan out each stage, and figure out the implications of the procedures in order to avoid unexpected headaches when you start work.

Order for building a raised pond
with brick walls and preformed liner

Job 3: Liner
Set the preformed liner in place, with the lip resting on the wall. Ensure that it is level.

Job 2: Inner wall
Build the inner wall, all the while checking its height in relation to the preformed liner.

Job 1: Footing
Dig out the footing for the inner and outer wall, level the site, lay hardpan, and put down a concrete slab.

Job 6: Finishing
Fill the pond with water. Top the walls with coping tiles bedded on mortar.

Job 5: Outer wall
Build the outer wall to finish level with the rim of the preformed liner.

Job 4: Fill cavity
Ease sand into the cavity around the liner so that it is well supported, particularly under the planting shelf.

Order for building a natural pond
with a flexible liner that is completely concealed

Job 1: Footing
Dig the hole and trenches for pipework. Lay the concrete footing for the wall.

Job 2: Butyl rubber liner
Spread synthetic padding in the hole and lay the liner.

Job 3: Brick wall
Build a wall around the pond (on liner), three bricks high.

Job 4: Trimming the liner
Run the liner up the outside of the wall. Trim it and fold on top of the wall.

Job 5: Finishing
Pack sand, then soil, against the outside of the wall. Spread soil over the wall and the planting shelf.

Have you got the time and energy?

Balance the time available against your energy level. If you are fit, with plenty of time on your hands, you can spread the tasks over weeks instead of days. But if you are short of time, you will need to speed up the procedures. Assuming that you already have good tools, one or more wheelbarrows, and plenty of buckets, the biggest single timesaver you can invest in is a cement mixer.

TOOLS AND MATERIALS

Although the choice of materials will depend upon the project, there are two guiding principles: it is always best to use the correct tools for the task, and it is always less expensive to purchase materials in bulk. It may be tempting to use a spade to shift sand rather than buying a new shovel, but it will take you twice as long, and your back will suffer. And don't fall for buying your sand in one prepacked bag at a time—it will be very expensive! (See page 10.)

GETTING QUOTES

You can cut costs by asking for quotes from local companies. List precisely what you want—name of product, size, color, and quantity—then call around for the best price. Never buy materials sight unseen: once you have the quotes, visit the suppliers and look at the products on offer. Having agreed on the price and the delivery date, it is preferable to pay only when the materials have been delivered.

VACATIONS

Make sure that your schedule takes national holidays into account. If you plan to work on a national holiday or a summer weekend, you must order the materials well ahead. You cannot expect companies to deliver on national holidays or in unsocial hours.

Delivery problems

Always assume that deliveries might be late, and order your materials well ahead. If you are ordering in bulk, can the truck park outside your gate? Are you allowed to unload materials on the land in front of your house, or will it pose a hazard? If a crane will be used to winch jumbo bags of sand or pallets of bricks off the truck, is there a convenient spot where they can be lifted over your fence?

TIMETABLE

If you are short of time, or asking friends to help (or paying for help), you must draw up a timetable. List the procedures and your expectations, and try to stick to completing the tasks in the allotted time. Build in some contingency time in case the weather turns ugly or there are other problems.

CALCULATING MATERIAL QUANTITIES

It is relatively easy to work out how many bricks you need for a particular job, but not quite so simple to decide on quantities for sand, Portland cement, and flexible liner. Order sand in bulk, because it is cheaper that way, and if any is left over, use it elsewhere in the garden. Portland cement is both expensive and short-lived, so order it a few bags at a time. The size of a flexible liner is a bit tricky to ascertain in advance, because you cannot be sure about dimensions until the hole has been dug and/or the walls built. As it is an expensive commodity, it is best to get on with the building work and take measurements directly from the project.

➔ *Work out the quantities, add on a little extra for good measure, and call at least three suppliers to check out prices.*

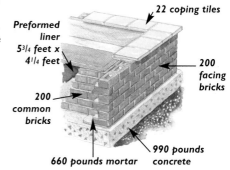

22 coping tiles

Preformed liner
5³⁄₄ feet x 4¹⁄₄ feet

200 facing bricks

200 common bricks

660 pounds mortar

990 pounds concrete

Guidelines for calculating quantities

Depending on the product, you need to work out the dimensions, the number of pieces, and/or the weight. Calculate the best number-to-price deal.

Hardpan ~ Usually sold by the truckload. Work out how much you need, order the amount to the nearest whole load above that amount, and then dig the footings deeper to use up the extra.

Gravel and sand ~ A whole truckload or jumbo bag is the cheapest option. Gift any left over to a neighbor.

Concrete ~ It's very difficult to work out how much you need. It is usually best to buy it one or two bags at a time, as and when it is needed.

Wall materials ~ Bricks and concrete blocks are usually sold by the pallet-load. Buy a complete load and plan to use the surplus on another project.

Flexible pond liner ~ Butyl rubber liners are very expensive. The best option is to take measurements directly from the hole or structure, and only to buy the absolute minimum. Some suppliers cut costs by selling precut sizes.

PROTECTING THE SURROUNDING AREA

If you are shifting soil and moving wheelbarrows over the lawn, it's a good idea to cover the grass with a plastic sheet or large sheets of plywood. If you are using a cement mixer, make sure that it is well away from the lawn and flowerbeds. Portland cement is corrosive and will kill plants and fish, so be careful how you use it. When doing repetitive tasks, such as walking from the cement mixer to the site, or using a wheelbarrow, try to vary the route, to avoid compacting the ground.

WILL YOU NEED SOME HELP?

Building ponds can be really good fun! If a friend or relative wants to help, why not agree? You will be giving the helper pleasure and spreading the workload. If your children or grandchildren want to help, let them join in with safe procedures and be prepared to watch over them. However, before letting grandchildren get involved, it is sensible to ask their parents' permission!

Remember that digging a hole and moving bricks are hard work. Are you fit enough for the tasks ahead? Check with your doctor if you have concerns.

Tools and materials

What do I need? Can I make any savings?

Tools and materials come from four main sources: home improvement stores for tools, bricks, blocks, and tiles, dedicated local suppliers for bulk items such as sand and gravel, and water garden specialists for all the fixtures and fittings. You can make savings—in money by purchasing materials in bulk, in time by using the correct tools for the job, and in effort by buying the best tools that you can afford. The following lists will show you the way.

GENERAL CONSTRUCTION TOOLS AND MACHINERY

Tools for measuring and marking

Pegs and string

Small tape measure

Carpenter's level

Big tape measure

Tools for moving materials

Gloves

Wheelbarrow

Bucket

Tools for digging, compacting, mixing, and raking

Spade

Shovel

Fork

Sledgehammer

Garden rake

Trowel

Tools for brick, stone, concrete, and mortar

Stonemason's hammer

Mason's trowel

Brick hammer

Grinder

Brick chisel

Pointing trowel

Cold chisel

Miscellaneous tools

Handsaw

Log saw

Jigsaw

Curved claw hammer

Rubber mallet

Drill bit (for wood and metal)

Power drill

Cordless drill

Masonry drill bit (for brick, concrete and stone)

Knife

Flat drill bit (for large holes in wood)

Scissors

Pliers

Tin snips

Screwdriver

Adjustable spanner

Paint brush

Machinery and power tool safety

Always follow the manufacturer's directions. Never use power tools if you are exhausted or taking medication. If the weather is wet or the lawn covered in dew, make sure that you use the tools in conjunction with a GFCI (Ground Fault Circuit Interrupter). Keep children out of harm's way.

RENTING TOOLS

If you are going to put down a concrete footing under a structure, you can easily cut time and effort in half by renting a power tamper to thump the hardpan into place. Mixing mortar and concrete by hand is undoubtedly a chore, but renting a cement mixer makes the task easy and enjoyable.

GENERAL CONSTRUCTION MATERIALS

Lining materials

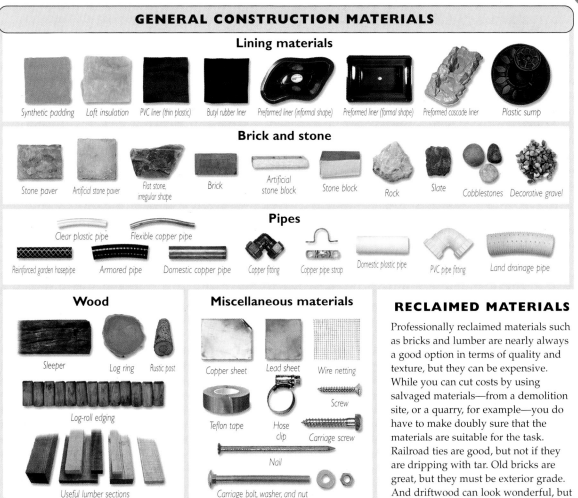

Synthetic padding | Loft insulation | PVC liner (thin plastic) | Butyl rubber liner | Preformed liner (informal shape) | Preformed liner (formal shape) | Preformed cascade liner | Plastic sump

Brick and stone

Stone paver | Artificial stone paver | Flat stone, irregular shape | Brick | Artificial stone block | Stone block | Rock | Slate | Cobblestones | Decorative gravel

Pipes

Clear plastic pipe | Flexible copper pipe

Reinforced garden hosepipe | Armored pipe | Domestic copper pipe | Copper fitting | Copper pipe strap | Domestic plastic pipe | PVC pipe fitting | Land drainage pipe

Wood

Sleeper | Log ring | Rustic post

Log-roll edging

Useful lumber sections

Miscellaneous materials

Copper sheet | Lead sheet | Wire netting

Teflon tape | Hose clip | Screw

Carriage screw

Nail

Carriage bolt, washer, and nut

RECLAIMED MATERIALS

Professionally reclaimed materials such as bricks and lumber are nearly always a good option in terms of quality and texture, but they can be expensive. While you can cut costs by using salvaged materials—from a demolition site, or a quarry, for example—you do have to make doubly sure that the materials are suitable for the task. Railroad ties are good, but not if they are dripping with tar. Old bricks are great, but they must be exterior grade. And driftwood can look wonderful, but not if its leaching salt into your pond!

CONCRETE AND MORTAR RECIPES

Do not use too much water, always use fresh Portland cement and hydrated lime, avoid using too much cement in the mortar, and use only clean, well-washed sand. In the recipe diagrams below, each oval represents one part.

Cement | Soft sand | Sharp sand | Gravel | Ballast | Lime

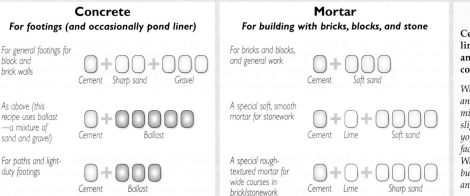

Concrete
For footings (and occasionally pond liner)

For general footings for block and brick walls

Cement + Sharp sand + Gravel

As above (this recipe uses ballast —a mixture of sand and gravel)

Cement + Ballast

For paths and light-duty footings

Cement + Ballast

Mortar
For building with bricks, blocks, and stone

For bricks and blocks, and general work

Cement + Soft sand

A special soft, smooth mortar for stonework

Cement + Lime + Soft sand

A special rough-textured mortar for wide courses in brick/stonework

Cement + Lime + Sharp sand

CAUTION

Cement powder, lime, wet concrete, and mortar are all corrosive!

Wear goggles, a mask, and gloves when mixing. If it is a hot or slightly breezy day, you must wash your face after mixing. Wear gloves while building with concrete and mortar.

Digging holes

What is the best way to tackle digging?

Inescapably, the construction of a pond involves digging a hole. Obviously, you need to be reasonably fit in order to cope with the work. To make digging easier, wear a comfortable pair of boots and a pair of gloves, use a spade that is just the right length and weight for you, and work at a steady, relaxed pace. There is something wonderfully therapeutic about pushing a sharp spade into slightly moist soil—it even smells good!

POINTS TO CONSIDER

- Is your site dry and sandy, hard and rocky, or wet and squashy? You need to dig a trial hole to find out.
- If the ground is very sandy, you must either resite the project or shore up the hole with plywood sheeting to stop the sides from caving in.
- If the ground is rocky, you might not need (or be able) to lay a footing.
- If the ground is waterlogged, you must either resite the project, or lay pipes underneath the footings to drain off the excess water.
- If, when you are digging, you come across an unexpected pipe or cable (it might be electricity, water, gas, sewage, oil, or land drains), you must stop work and check it out.

CROSS-SECTIONS

A cross-section is a vertical slice through a project, right down to the footing. Draw a cross-section to help you to visualize how components fit together.

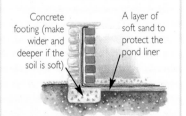

Concrete footing (make wider and deeper if the soil is soft)

A layer of soft sand to protect the pond liner

1. Check your measurements ~ You must measure the thickness of the various materials—for example, bricks, mortar courses, footings—so that you know how deep to dig the hole.

2. Draw to scale ~ Draw cross-sections to scale so that you have a clear understanding of the various layers and the order of work.

MARKING OUT POND SHAPES

Pond with a preformed liner in an irregular shape

← Position the preformed liner on the ground and align it as required. Look straight down past the edge of the liner and use chalk to mark around the profile on the ground. Run a second line around the first, about a spade-width away.

Creating natural or irregular shapes

← Decide how long and wide you want the pond to be, and use pegs to mark out these points on the ground. Use a rope or hosepipe to link up the points until you have the envisaged shape. Use chalk, trailed hydrated lime, or marker spray paint to define the line of cut.

Rectangular shapes

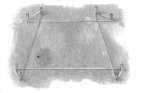

← Decide on the alignment. Use a tape measure, pegs, and string to set out the approximate rectangle on the ground. Measure the diagonals and make gradual adjustments to one or all of the pegs until both diagonal measurements are identical and the strings are taut.

Removing turf

Use a tape measure, pegs, and string to mark out the area on the ground. Take a spade and slice up the area into a spade-width grid. Hold the spade at a low angle and slice under the turf to remove one square. Repeat across the whole area.

LEVELS AND DEPTHS

To create a level area on the ground, start by banging in a peg at the lowest point. Run a string to the higher ground and bang in another peg. Bridge the two pegs with a length of wood and check with a carpenter's level. Repeatedly lower the ground along the line of the string, tapping in the second peg until both pegs and ground are at the same level. Work outward from these points with additional pegs.

Check the depth of a hole by using a tape to measure straight down from a length of wood bridging the pegs.

TRENCHES, PLANTING SHELVES, AND SLOPES FOR PONDS

Trenches

↘ A retaining wall for a pond is constructed in a trench. Level the site and slice away the topsoil. Mark off a stick with the depth and width measurements of the trench. Dig out a flat-bottomed, clean-sided trench, all the while using the stick to check your progress.

Planting shelves

↓ Planting shelves are designed to hold marginal plants around the fringes of a pond. Decide on the width and depth of the shelf, and its alignment to the sun. Mark the width, depth, and shape of the shelf, and dig out the soil. Sculpt the shelf so that it slopes upward to the edge of the pond.

Slopes

↙ The sides of the hole need to be sculpted from the inner edge of the planting shelf toward the central and deepest part of the pond. They need to slope down at a 3-in-1 angle (see slope ratios below). At this angle, the soil and loose sand under the liner will not shift.

Cross-section of a pond with a flexible liner

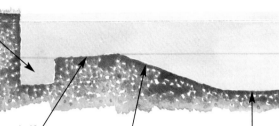

Trench
Dig a trench, making it deep and wide enough to take a concrete footing and the number of brick courses that constitute the retaining wall.

Planting shelf
Shape the shelf so that it is wide and deep enough to take a good range of marginal plants. The recommended depth is up to about 8 inches.

Slope
Sculpt the slope so that the soil and sand under the liner stay put. If the soil rolls, it is too steep.

Bottom
Should be broad and flat.

SLOPE RATIOS

The ideal angle for the side-to-bottom slope of a natural pond is 3-in-1. This means that for every three units of horizontal measurement, the vertical depth increases by a single unit.

DISPOSING OF SOIL

Digging holes creates waste soil. Topsoil is too precious to throw away and can always be put to good use somewhere in the garden. Subsoil, which is sterile, can be employed at the base of a decorative bank or raised border, banked around the edge of the pond, or used to build up an area for a waterfall or rockery. Try and plan the whole disposal exercise so that the soil gets moved only once, from the hole to its final destination in the garden.

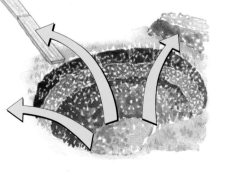

Create a feature adjacent to the pond
To build a bank around the edge of the pond, put the topsoil to one side, then dig out the pond and directly use the subsoil to create the bank. Leave several weeks for it to settle, then bring back the topsoil and cover it.

Create a feature elsewhere in the garden
Lay a line of workboards from the pond to the area set aside for the feature, so that you can use the wheelbarrow without damaging the garden.

Remove from the garden completely
Keep the topsoil. Decide on the shortest possible route from the pond to the gate and lay a line of workboards for the wheelbarrow.

DIGGERS

One way to help with excavation is to rent a small digger. Certainly a digger will get the task done fast, but will your gates be wide enough? Will a digger compact the lawn and scrape the drive? Will it be able to turn and maneuver without doing damage to the borders, trees, and all the other features? If the pond is medium-size, it is probably easier to ask friends and family to help and dig it by hand.

If you are planning a really large pond and digging by hand is simply not an option, you have the choice of renting a digger and getting down to the task yourself, or renting a digger plus driver. Find a local contractor and get a written price quote. Write down what you want—the position of the pond, its depth, where you want the soil to be placed, how you want the topsoil to be saved and put to one side, and so on. Specify clearly what you expect and what you do not want to happen. If you want the contractor to lay down workboards to protect the lawn, then say so. Make sure that the contractor is fully insured before confirming the job.

Building walls

What are the options if I need to build a wall?

Ponds and water features often require walls—for example, an ornamental and functional wall to surround a raised pond, or a concealed retaining wall to support a natural-looking pond. You can build with concrete blocks, brick, or stone. Concrete blocks are cheap but heavy, ugly, and not very adaptable. Stone is expensive, attractive, and has more potential. Brick is reasonably low-cost, easy to handle, and very flexible. Consider the structure, style, your skills, and budget.

POINTS TO CONSIDER

- Will the wall be hidden from view—for example, the inner wall of a raised pond, or the buried wall around a natural pond?
- Is the wall primarily decorative rather than functional?
- Is the wall going to be straight, broadly curved, or tightly curved?
- If the wall is on show, does it need to complement existing brick or stone structures such as the house, patio, or garden walls?
- Do you have to work to a tight budget, or is money no object?
- If you want to build walls using large components, such as big pieces of stone, is there comfortable access to the garden with easy parking in the road, a wide gate, and level walkways?
- Decide which materials to use after answering the above questions.

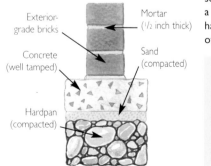

For the walls of a raised pond, choose materials that complement the house or nearby garden walls. This pond has new exterior-grade bricks topped with concrete "quarry" tiles.

Wall basics

Thick walls are more stable than thin ones. High walls need to be thicker than low ones. High, thick walls need wide, deep footings. If only one side of a wall is on show, the hidden side can be made from low-cost concrete blocks.

FOOTINGS

Walls need footings in order to remain stable and firm. If you are building a low, three-brick-high retaining wall for a natural pond (a wall that is going to be buried), the footing needs only to be a series of good-size shovelfuls of concrete laid directly on top of a trench full of hardpan.

If the wall is to stand above ground, dig a trench to a depth of 12 inches, making it 12 inches wide. Put 6 inches of compacted hardpan in the trench, followed by 3/4 inch of compacted sand. Top off with 5 1/4 inches of well-tamped concrete. If the ground is hard and dry, the hardpan does not have to be so thick. If it is wet and soft, dig a deeper trench and use more hardpan and a greater depth of concrete.

Exterior-grade bricks

Mortar (1/2 inch thick)

Concrete (well tamped)

Sand (compacted)

Hardpan (compacted)

CONCRETE MIX

A good ratio is 1–2–3: 1 part of Portland cement to 2 parts of sharp sand and 3 parts of washed gravel. Once laid down, the concrete must be covered up to protect it from rain, sun, and frost while curing.

USING MORTAR

Unlike Portland cement, which can be purchased ready-mixed, mortar has to be mixed on site. Depending upon the amount needed, you can mix a small amount in a wheelbarrow, a sizeable pile on a workboard, or a slightly larger heap in a cement mixer.

As mixing mortar and building walls are activities that use different muscles—they are both hard work but in different ways—the best plan of action is to balance the activities by working to a rhythm: mix a little, clean up, build a little, clean up, and so on.

MORTAR MIX

A good mix is 1–1–6: 1 part Portland cement to 1 part hydrated lime and 6 parts soft sand. Hydrated lime gives a creamy, easy-to-use texture that is good for brick and stone work (see page 17).

HOW TO BUILD BRICK WALLS

Bricks have six sides: two end or "header" faces, two side or "stretcher" faces, a top or "frog" face, and a bottom face. Most walls are built with the bricks set frog-face uppermost, so that the stretcher or header faces are on view. Each row of bricks is called a course.

The pattern of bricks is termed the bond. The object of the bond is to stagger the vertical joints in order to create a strong wall. Most of the projects in this book are built using a running bond to create either a single-brick or double-brick wall. It is usual to build the corners or "quoins" first, setting them vertically using a carpenter's level and line.

Step 6
Bed the coping tiles on a generous layer of mortar.

Step 5
Use a small trowel to tool the joints and to generally tidy up the face of the wall.

Step 4
Adjust the mortar thickness under the top course so that the two sides of the wall are level.

Metal peg for holding a guide string level

Step 1
Lay the first course of bricks (placing both bricks if a double-brick wall). Make sure they are well aligned and spaced.

Step 2
Continue building the courses. Make sure that the corners are horizontally and vertically square.

Step 3
Make repeated checks with the carpenter's level as the wall progresses, ensuring that it is vertically and horizontally level.

How to finish the top of the wall

The top of a wall is finished by a coping, the function of which is to bring the wall to a visual conclusion and to deflect rain away from the wall. Traditional styles of coping include tiles bedded in mortar, and bricks set side by side on their stretcher face.

STONE WALLS

Stone walls are built like brick walls, with the stones bedded in mortar, and are usually built up from thin, flat pieces, like plates stacked in a heap. Although you can use sawn stone, it is both difficult to find and expensive.

If it is necessary to cut stone, use found pieces of a type that splits down into easy-to-use, square-faced pieces. Support the stone on a piece of old carpet, and use a stonemason's hammer with a brick chisel for general cutting, or a cold chisel for more delicate work.

If possible, use local stone (or reconstituted stone that looks like natural local stone). This ensures that the structure will harmonize with buildings in the area.

CIRCULAR WALLS

Base board weighted by bricks. Trammel raised as the wall grows

Trammel—length of wood with a nail one end on which to pivot; distance from the nail to the end is the radius

Trammel method (see below)

The smaller the building unit (brick or block), the easier it is to build a circular wall. The traditional method of building a circle with a small diameter is to use a piece of easy-to-make apparatus called a trammel, pivoted on a nail that marks the center of the circle. The trammel (like the hand of a clock) ensures that the radius is constant.

Mosaic

Mosaics are decorative designs made by sticking small pieces of a material (such as tiles, glass, pebbles, or shells) to a flat surface to create a two-dimensional picture or pattern. The design is drawn onto the surface, and each area is spread with plaster or Portland cement, then the mosaic pieces are pressed into place.

OTHER MATERIALS

Low walls can be built from just about everything—railroad ties, sawn wood, logs, concrete blocks, scrap iron, old crates, metal containers, driftwood, glass bricks, empty wine bottles, compacted soil, molded concrete, and many other found and natural materials. However, you must ensure that the walls are structurally sound as well as decorative.

So, if you are adventurous and want to use a material in an exciting way for low walls (no more than about 24 inches high), check first that you won't infringe zoning regulations and that the walls will not pose a health hazard. Then if family and neighbors have no objections, go ahead and see how it works out.

Lining ponds and water features

What is the best material to choose for the liner?

A liner is best defined as the waterproof layer that ensures that the pond or water feature is watertight. At one time, ponds were lined with puddled wet clay (clay that was pressed into place with the feet), but now they may be lined with concrete, plastic sheet, butyl rubber sheet, preformed fiberglass, or preformed plastic. The choice of liner will depend upon the size and shape of the feature, how long you want it to last, and how much you want to spend.

WHICH LINER IS BEST?

➥ For a low-cost pond, which you do not regard as a permanent feature, PVC is perfect. If you want a pond to last for 25 years, butyl rubber is a better choice. A preformed liner is ideal for a raised pond. Carefully consider all the options in the light of your needs, and then make your choice.

Pond with irregular shape	Geometric pond	Canal	Bubbler fountain	Reservoir tank
Butyl rubber	**Preformed**	**Butyl rubber**	**Sump**	**Pond paint**
Butyl rubber sheet is best for large ponds with an irregular shape—you can order it in any size.	Small, geometric ponds—raised or sunken—are best made with preformed liners.	Butyl rubber comes in rolls—perfect for long, narrow water features such as canals and cascades.	Preformed plastic sumps are designed for bubbler fountains and small pump-and-sump features.	Pond paint is really good for small, cement-rendered brick tanks and cisterns.

FLEXIBLE LINERS: BUTYL AND PVC

Butyl rubber and PVC need to be handled with care, because they will be rendered totally useless if they are torn or punctured. Ideally, this type of liner needs to be sandwiched between two layers of synthetic padding, and then either protected by the structure, or at least hidden from view. With a bit of planning, it is possible to build a double-walled pond with the flexible liner running under the base slab and up between the two walls, in such a way that the liner is totally hidden and protected, both from the harmful effects of sunlight and from accidental damage.

Durability

PVC rubber is thin and will last for about five years. Butyl rubber is thick and guaranteed to last for at least 25 years. Thicker liners are less prone to puncturing.

For a sunken pond *(irregular shape)*

Here the liner (shown in black) runs under and up the back of the retaining wall. Synthetic padding is shown in green.

For a raised pond *(irregular or rectangular)*

Here the liner (shown in black) is sandwiched in the retaining wall. Synthetic padding is shown in green.

PREFORMED LINERS

Preformed liners are perfect both for small raised ponds and sunken ponds, whether a geometrical or natural shape.

There are two types: the expensive, smooth-sided fiberglass liner that will last many years, and the rather saggy PVC liner that might last only four to five years. The secret of success with a preformed liner is to provide it with plenty of structural support—a firm concrete slab base, plenty of soft sand pushed between the liner and the surrounding ground or structure, and a capping of tiles or slabs to protect the vulnerable rim.

For a sunken pond *(circular, square, or irregular)*

This small liner is bedded on sand. If the edges of the pond are to be surrounded by rocks, these will need to be supported by concrete.

For a raised pond *(circular or rectangular)*

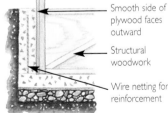

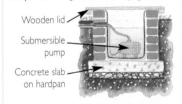

This liner is bedded on compacted sand over a concrete footing, and the sides supported by sand.

Limitations

Preformed liners are limited both by their small size and by the selection of fixed shapes available. So if you want to build a large pond to your own design, they are not much use.

TRADITIONAL CONCRETE AND RENDER

Concrete liner, method 1 *(plastering method)*

Concrete ponds predate more modern options. They involve quite a bit of work, but some people will find this enjoyable. This method is a good choice for shallow natural ponds. Line the sides of the hole with wire netting. Mix the concrete to a stiff consistency and throw it at the sides of the pond until there is a build-up of concrete poking through the netting. Use a wood float to give the concrete a smooth finish, then cover with plastic and leave to dry out slowly.

Concrete liner, method 2
(shuttering method)

A good choice for a square sunken pond. Dig out a flat-bottomed, square hole. Pour 6 inches of concrete into the hole and tamp it to a smooth, level finish. When it is dry, build a plywood box 8 inches away from the sides of the hole, with the smooth sides facing the soil. Fill the cavity with concrete to form the pond's walls.

Smooth side of plywood faces outward

Structural woodwork

Wire netting for reinforcement

Keep costs low by using "shuttering grade" plywood to make the box.

Rendering brick, block, and stone walls

Mix a quantity of cement-rich mortar. Dampen the walls. Use a wooden float to skim the mortar over the walls until you have a thickness of 1¼ inches. Work from bottom to top until the walls are completely covered with render. When the mortar has stiffened, use a magnesium float to work the render to a smooth finish. Finally, wait 48 hours and brush pond paint over the render.

SUMPS

A sump is a reservoir that feeds a pump. A traditional sump is a small brick box, the sides of which are rendered and coated in pond paint. Alternatively, preformed plastic sumps are readily available (see page 19).

Wooden lid

Submersible pump

Concrete slab on hardpan

OTHER LINING METHODS

If you have a lot of clay in your garden, you can use it to line a small, shallow, natural pond. Dig up the clay and remove all the stones. With the clay still wet, smear a thick layer of it over the pond and paddle it with your feet until it is a well-trodden, homogeneous mass. Allow the clay to dry until it is a damp, cheesy consistency and fill the pond with water. On no account let the clay dry out and crack. The thicker the clay, the better.

Pumps and filters

How do I choose the right pump for the job?

Pumps are used to move water. If you want to run water from one pond to another, or through a fountain, or up to the level of a waterfall, you are going to need an electric pump. Choose a low-voltage submersible pump that is powerful enough for the water feature in question. Depending upon the size of the pump, the type of water feature and its situation, and whether fish are going to be present, you may need a water filter in conjunction with the pump.

Average-sized pump
For small ponds and water features

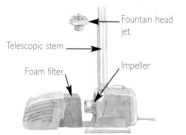

A small, low-voltage pump complete with a telescopic stem, a fountain head jet, and an integral filter to protect moving parts.

Pump basics

Things to consider (see also Pump power box, to work out the size of pump needed):

- How many gallons of water do you want to move per minute/hour?

- What is the head height (the vertical distance from the surface of the water to the fountain head jet)? The greater the head height and the higher the water is required to spurt, the bigger the pump needed.

- Do you need a special filtration system to protect fish?

Separate filter
For large ponds

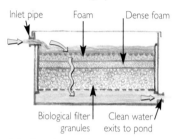

A dual mechanical-biological filter system, with foam filters for solids and a biological filter for water purification.

ELECTRICITY AND SAFETY

- *Always fit a GFCI between the pump and the power supply, to protect yourself from electric shock.*

- *Make sure that the electrics (all cables and outlets) are designed for outside use.*

- *It is good practice to avoid putting your hands in the water when the power is on, even if there is a GFCI.*

FOUNTAIN SET-UP

The most common set-up is called direct installation, where the fountain head leads straight off a pump via an extending tube, or where the pump is directly beneath a statuette. Indirect installation is less common: it uses a remote pump and is less efficient but easier to maintain. To install a statuette fountain (a sculpture with built-in water pipe and fountain head attachment), sit the pump on a level base, then build a plinth for the statuette and use riser pipe to connect the pump to the base of the statuette fountain. (See pages 48–49 for more about fountains.)

Fountains and plants

Some plants are unhappy if they are sprayed with water, especially plants with broad leaves such as water-lilies. If this presents a problem, locate the plants outside the spray area.

PUMP POWER

The greater the head height and spray height (see box on Pump basics), the higher the flow rate needed. Calculate the flow rate of a pump by timing how long it takes to fill a container of known capacity— if it takes 10 minutes to fill 50 gallons, the flow rate is 300 gallons per hour.

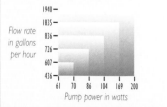

Flow rate in gallons per hour

1940 —
1835 —
836 —
726 —
607 —
436 —

61 70 86 104 169 200

Pump power in watts

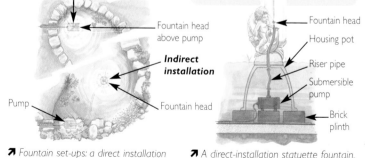

↗ Fountain set-ups: a direct installation and an indirect installation with the pump on the banks of the pond.

↗ A direct-installation statuette fountain. Bricks and a pot are used to raise the statuette to the correct level.

SUMP SET-UP

A "hat" sump is a preformed plastic reservoir, used to hold enough water to feed a pump. The pump sits in the sump, where it pushes water up through the chosen water feature, such as a fountain or sculpture. Sumps are inexpensive and easy to install.

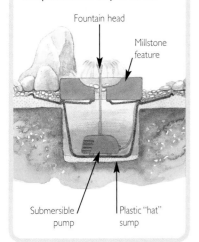

Fountain head

Millstone feature

Submersible pump

Plastic "hat" sump

WATERFALL SET-UP

Water supply pipe

Rocks arranged to give a naturalistic effect

Header pool

Filter

Run-off shelf

Power cable

Pump

A waterfall is really just a body of water falling off a shelf. A garden waterfall is made up from a large reservoir or sump, a pump, and a header pool complete with a run-off shelf. The pump pushes water from the reservoir up to the header pool, where it overflows and runs off the shelf back into the reservoir pool. The waterfall can be a self-contained sump feature or part of a larger pond and stream scheme. (See pages 50–51.)

Remember

- *The larger the pump and the greater the width of the run-off shelf, the more dynamic the waterfall.*

- *Most plants are unhappy under falling or moving water.*

POND PUMP AND FILTER SET-UP

Small submersible pumps have their own integral foam filter to protect the moving parts. Large fishponds and plantless ornamental ponds require an external mechanical-biological filter bed to ensure the quality of the water. At some point in the circulation, the water drains through a foam material where the solids are removed. Once strained, the water flows over a biological filter that encourages positive bacteria, and then on through the outlet pipe.

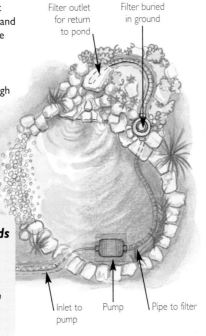

Filter outlet for return to pond

Filter buried in ground

Inlet to pump

Pump

Pipe to filter

Other filtration methods

- *Large ponds can be protected by building traditional rock, sand, and charcoal filter beds.*

- *Fishponds can be protected with an ultraviolet radiation filter, to ensure that the water stays crystal clear.*

PUMP CONNECTORS AND FIXINGS

The greater the power of the pump, the larger the diameter of the various pipes and fittings. If you decide to change a fitting, check that the diameter matches. Though the water supply pipes are ribbed so that they resist kinking, always lay them in broad curves or fit elbow fittings. Make sure that all the fixings are compatible both with the pump size and with the screw threads.

CLEANING PUMPS AND FILTERS

Check the equipment once a week. For an average pump, turn off the power, lift the pump from the water, unclip the filter cover, and remove the foam filter. Wash the whole thing in warm water.

If you have a separate filter, first remove the foam and brushes from the chamber and wash them in water. Lift the basket of biological glass, plastic, and ceramic filters clear of the chamber. Don't be tempted to remove the algae, because this forms part of the natural cleaning process—just remove the debris and clean out the chamber.

Water pipes and power cables

What sort of pipework is required?

If a pond has a filter system or contains a fountain, an electric pump and pipes to conduct the water need to be installed. Water features have the same requirements. Power cables need to be protected by pipes. Mostly, all pipes are buried to hide them from view. The easiest option is to use ribbed **PVC** pipe, also called armored pipe, for both purposes. It will bend around broad curves without kinking, but to fit around tight corners, pipe joints are essential.

CONSIDERATIONS

Requirements ~ Will the pipework be buried, hidden from view, or on display?

Appearance ~ If a pipe is going to be on show, are you happy with ribbed PVC pipe, or would you prefer to use small-bore PVC or copper? Do you want the pipework to form a decorative part of the design, such as a copper or lead spout?

Safety ~ Is the pipework going to be run under active areas of the garden (areas that are going to be worked with a spade or fork)?

Maintenance and re-installation ~ Do you want to be able to withdraw the power cables or to inspect the water pipes?

Protect yourself by using a GFCI

For safety's sake, all garden electrics need to be fitted with a GFCI or ground fault circuit interrupter, commonly known as a safety cut-out. This inexpensive and completely necessary device ensures that the power is instantly cut off if the cable is damaged by accident.

METHODS FOR INSTALLING WATER PIPES AND CABLE PIPES

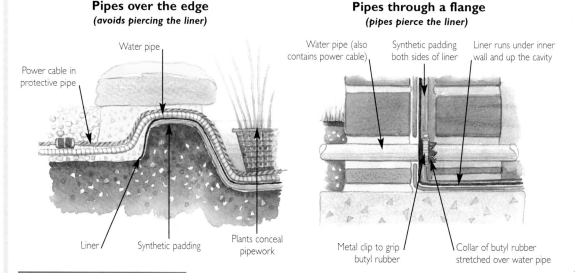

Pipes over the edge
(avoids piercing the liner)

Water pipe

Power cable in protective pipe

Liner

Synthetic padding

Plants conceal pipework

Pipes through a flange
(pipes pierce the liner)

Water pipe (also contains power cable)

Synthetic padding both sides of liner

Liner runs under inner wall and up the cavity

Metal clip to grip butyl rubber

Collar of butyl rubber stretched over water pipe

PROTECTING CABLES

It is a good idea to double-protect cables by passing them through a pipe and then covering the pipe (in its trench) with a layer of old roof tiles. This guards against accidental damage by garden fork or spade.

↖↗ When you have gone to a lot of trouble making sure that your pond is watertight, it is better not to cut holes in it for the pipes carrying water and the power cable. The simplest option is to pass the pipework up and over the edge of the pond at a point where it can be hidden from view. If the pipework has to go through the pond wall, the method used depends on the pond's construction. If the liner is butyl rubber, cut a very small hole for the pipe (so the pipe is a very tight fit) and fit a clip around the resultant butyl rubber flange. For less flexible liners, use a tank connection complete with nuts, bolts, gaskets, and sealant.

EXAMPLES OF PIPEWORK

Simple pond fountain set-up
concealed under a plinth installation

→ The pump is installed on a concrete slab and covered with a housing (either a large, upturned flowerpot or a purpose-built brick chamber). The statuette sits on the housing, with a riser pipe running down from the underside to link up with the pump.

Statuette

Adjustment valve

Upturned flowerpot

Pump

EXTENDING CABLES

All cables, fixtures, and fittings must be designed for outside use, and the cables protected by armored pipes. Fit a circuit breaker. Prior to making alterations, switch off the power at the service panel. If you have any doubts at all about your skills, ask a professional electrician to do the job.

A pump and separate filter set-up
with filter outside the pond

→ The filter chamber is set up at the side of the pond, either hidden in a shrubbery or in a little purpose-built shed. The filter must be installed at the highest point in the system—higher than both the pump and the pond. The pump pushes water from the pond up into the filter chamber, where it runs through the filter foam to remove solids, on through the biological filter to encourage positive bacteria, and down and out through the outlet pipe. When the water has passed through the filter, it is clean enough to go back into the pond.

  The rule for positioning a surface filter chamber such as this is to place the filter as far away from the pump as possible, so that the clean water has time to disperse around the pond. If the pump and the filter outlet are too close together, there is a danger that the clean, filtered water will be instantly sucked back through the filter, and other parts of the pond consequently never get filtered.

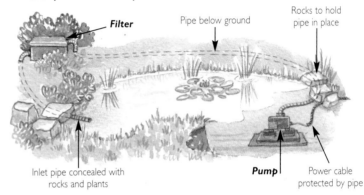

Filter

Pipe below ground

Rocks to hold pipe in place

Inlet pipe concealed with rocks and plants

Pump

Power cable protected by pipe

A stand-alone water feature with sump
and a small pump

→ With small, stand-alone water features, such as millstones and mini fountains, the pump is installed directly in a small plastic sump, where it is covered by the feature. The power cable snakes out of the sump to be concealed by rocks or plants.

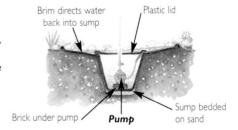

Brim directs water back into sump

Plastic lid

Brick under pump

Pump

Sump bedded on sand

Solar power

If you like the idea of a pond with a small fountain, yet the site is a long way from a power source, or you simply don't want to be bothered with lots of cables snaking about the garden, consider a small, self-contained, solar-powered fountain. While these are good for many situations, such as small raised ponds and remote ponds, the downside is that currently the integral solar collectors are rather bulky and unsightly. They work only in full sunlight, well away from overhanging trees.

HIDING PIPES WITH ROCKS AND PLANTS

In situations where pipes cannot be buried (such as on an established patio, or perhaps a roof garden), they can be artfully concealed by rocks, pots, bricks, and plants. The best plan of action is to set up your water feature, live with it for a few weeks, and then consider carefully how the pipework can be hidden from view. You could build a mini rockery, or set the pipes well back against a wall and screen them with a line of pot plants.

MAKING PIPES PART OF THE DESIGN

The project can be shaped so that the outflow from the filter chamber to the pond takes the form of an open rill or even a canal with traditional clay or stone gulleys. You could use pipes that are attractive in their own right—copper, lead, brass, or stainless steel. With patio features, flexible small-bore copper tube can be employed for the whole circuit, so that the copper is a positive part of the design.

Shapes and styles

The shape, size, and location of your garden will, to a great extent, dictate the form, scale, and position of a pond within your garden. However, the style of the pond—whether it is big, small, informal, formal, raised, sunken, Japanese, wildlife, and with or without a pump and fountains—is something only you can decide. Spend time visiting parks, water gardens, and historic mansions in order to broaden your appreciation of the possible options.

POINTS TO CONSIDER

Walk around your garden and decide on the pond's orientation, taking into account the way the sun moves around the garden. Bear in mind the fact that unlike a flower border, which you can easily replant to suit your changing likes and dislikes, a pond is a more permanent feature.

Look at the total shape and size of your garden and list all the things that you want to keep. Consider the lifestyle of your family and the way the garden is used at weekends. Have a family meeting and consider all the possible options. Compile a list of requirements, and then, working from that starting point, begin to draw out a detailed plan.

- Does the proposed project blend comfortably into the shape of your garden, or are you trying to force it to fit?
- Do you envisage listening to the soft sounds of a fountain?
- Would you like a wildlife pond complete with frogs and toads, and lots of mud? Do you want lots of vegetation?
- Ideally, would the pond be almost maintenance-free? Or do you like the idea of looking after pumps and sumps?
- Do you like rock and gravel, grass, decking, or tiles?
- Do you want the pond to be in a particular style, such as Japanese, for example?
- Should you consider the safety of children or older people?

POND SHAPES

The shape, function, and structure of a pond go hand in hand. For example, if you want a crisp, tiled pond, build from brick or stone, rather than unsupported butyl rubber.

Consider the proposed shape and location of the pond in relation to the size of your garden, and then look at the structural options and see if it is possible.

Sunken ponds

Sunken ponds can be any shape you like. Flexible butyl rubber is the most versatile liner to use, because it enables you to build a whole host of shapes with ease.

Geometric

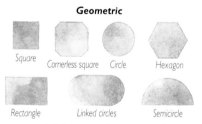

Square   Cornerless square   Circle   Hexagon

Rectangle   Linked circles   Semicircle

While squares and circles are easier than complicated geometrical forms, they all require a lot of building expertise.

Irregular   *Combination*

The easiest of all options—just dig an irregular hole, then edge it with brick and line it with flexible butyl rubber.

Use rendered brick for the square pond, brick and butyl rubber for the irregular pond.

Raised ponds

Raised ponds are often geometrical in shape and formal in design, and made from brick or stone lined with mortar or butyl rubber, because it is easier to build them that way.

Geometric   *Irregular*   *Combination*

A small, square pond made using a preformed liner faced with brick.

A kidney-shaped pond made using a preformed liner faced with wood.

A stepped pond with waterfall, built from brick lined with butyl rubber.

Sunken and raised combinations

A combination sunken pond complete with a waterfall can be built with a preformed liner faced with brick for the raised header pool, and brick lined with butyl rubber for the main pond.

POND STYLES

The style of pond has to be sympathetic to the style of the garden and its location. Formal ponds are usually geometrical and clearly defined—a good choice for a city garden. A small, Japanese pond with a minute water feature can look equally good in a paved city courtyard. Larger rural gardens have more scope: a pond can blend with the overall theme of the garden, or you can make a special garden "room" in a particular style, with a pond as its focus.

↑ A rectangular pond set within a lawn and alongside an old-fashioned herringbone brick patio, which makes an ideal vantage point for observing the fish. Informal planting edges the grassy banks and spills on to the patio.

↑ A small, circular, low-maintenance pond, designed as part of a large patio. The grouped pot plants break up the formality and provide some shade for the fish. This pond could also be surrounded by stone pavers or set in the middle of a lawn.

← A wildlife pond complete with a beach, bog garden, and rockery. A concrete ring footing was built for a brick retaining wall around a pond lined with synthetic padding and butyl rubber. The clients were passionate about wildlife—fish, frogs, and plants—and wanted this pond to fill the garden to capacity.

→ The clients wanted a small pond for their petite, well-established Japanese garden. Their choice of form and materials (a sunken pond, feature rocks, gravel beach, and restrained planting) was dictated by the desire for characteristic Japanese imagery. The end result is a beautiful, easycare pond, which is perfect for a small city garden.

More style notes

The style must relate to the size of the site and the "mood" you are creating.

- If you want a wildlife pond, this imposes few limits—it could be a Japanese pond, a romantic pond complete with classical references, a pond with a bog garden close to the house—anything is possible.

- If you like order, formality, and classical symmetry, opt for an integrated scheme complete with a patio, formal pond, and steps.

- If you want a sense of urgency and excitement, choose a style that incorporates moving water, such as a tumbling stream, canal with a waterfall, or a classical wall spout.

- You could have a design based on circles—a circular pond, circular flowerbed, and circular patio.

Ponds with flexible liners

Flexible liners look difficult to fit. Is that the case?

Of all the methods of building a pond, using a flexible liner is the easiest. It could be argued that there are extra problems when it comes to sorting out the edges—especially when building a raised pond, or an informal pond with planting around the edges—but against that, a flexible liner enables you to build just about any shape of pond that captures your imagination. If you want to build something a little out of the ordinary, this is the method to choose.

WHAT IS FLEXIBLE LINER?

This is a sheet material available in rolls or pre-sized packs. Sizes range from 27 feet square to 100 feet x 65 feet. Polyethylene is the least durable, PVC is stronger, and butyl rubber lasts longest.

Sunken pond or raised pond?
Flexible liners are suitable for both sunken and raised ponds. A flexible liner is perfect for a wildlife pond; the trick is to design and build the pond so that the liner is hidden from view as far as possible. Raised ponds are slightly more difficult to build.

Shape, style, and scale
PVC and butyl rubber come in rectilinear sheets, so the most economical option is to build a rectilinear pond.

If you build a circular or free-form wildlife pond, the big triangular offcuts of liner produced can be used as extra

ADVANTAGES AND DISADVANTAGES

Advantages

✔ The pond can be any size or shape.

✔ Flexible liners are the most economical.

✔ You can choose a flexible liner to suit your budget.

✔ You get a guarantee to match your outlay—5 years for the cheapest, right up to 35 years for quality butyl rubber.

Disadvantages

✘ Flexible liners can easily be punctured by roots or by carelessness.

✘ A deep pond means that there will be a lot of tucks in the liner at the edges.

✘ The liner requires a lot of preparation and substructure, especially under the planting shelves and edges: concrete footings, brick walls, and padding on one or both sides.

FLEXIBLE LINER OPTIONS

pieces of padding under heavy fountains, or better still as liners under areas of bog garden.

If you want a deep circular or free-form pond, you have to accept that there will be lots of wrinkles and tucks at the sides and edges, where the liner comes up the sides of the pond and over the rim. The best way of overcoming this problem is to design the pond so that the edges of the liner are completely hidden from view—either under soil, boulders, a beach, heavy stone slabs, bricks, or grass. The deeper the pond in relation to its diameter, the greater the difficulty.

Choosing liner material

Polyethylene ~ The cheapest option, only suitable for very small ponds. Use padding and it will last for 3–5 years.

PVC ~ A low-cost option. If you buy the best, use padding, and follow all the directions, it will last up to 15 years.

Butyl rubber ~ Butyl rubber is twice as expensive as PVC, but is guaranteed to last for between 25–35 years. This is the product to select if you want the pond to last. It also requires padding.

CALCULATING AREAS OF LINER AND PADDING

Let's say that the pond is 15 feet long, 12 feet wide and 3 feet deep. Calculate the total length of the liner by doubling the depth and adding on the length measurement plus 3 feet. This gives you a total length of 24 feet. Find the total width by doubling the depth measurement and adding on the width measurement plus 3 feet. This gives you a total width of 21 feet. You need a liner measuring 24 feet x 21 feet, a total of 504 square feet.

THE IMPORTANCE OF PADDING

Padding protects the liner from sharp objects such as roots and pointed stones. If the liner is to be hidden under a heavy weight (rocks or soil), padding is needed on both sides.

Synthetic padding ~ A long-lasting synthetic padding, rather like the padding that was once used under carpets. It is designed to protect the liner from being pierced by stones and roots, and from penetration caused by the weight of the water pushing the liner down on to gritty subsoil. The guarantees for some liners require that they are used in conjunction with a good-quality synthetic padding.

Alternatives to synthetic padding ~ There are many alternatives to using synthetic padding, such as soft sand, roofing insulation, carpet padding, old carpet, or newspaper, but it doesn't make sense to put an expensive liner at risk by economizing.

BUILDING PONDS WITH A FLEXIBLE LINER

Sunken pond with an irregular shape and natural edge

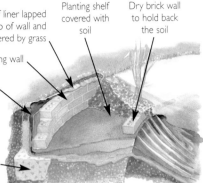

Edge of liner lapped over top of wall and covered by grass

Planting shelf covered with soil

Dry brick wall to hold back the soil

Brick retaining wall

Liner sandwiched between two layers of synthetic padding

Concrete ring footing for the wall

↗ A wildlife pond complete with a planting shelf for marginals.

Sunken pond with an irregular shape and brick edge

Synthetic padding and liner spread over the site, run up the outside of the wall, and folded under coping

Brick retaining wall, one brick thick

Decorative brick coping

Planting shelf with soil

Sand packed in cavity between wall and soil

Single row of bricks (laid on mortar) to hold back the soil

Concrete ring footing (6 inches thick, built on top of liner) to support brick wall

Extra piece of synthetic padding on top of liner

↗ A semiformal sunken pond with a visible brick edging and a planting shelf.

Rectangular sunken pond with brick edge

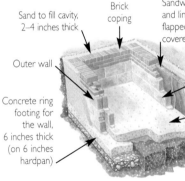

Sand to fill cavity, 2–4 inches thick

Brick coping

Sandwich of synthetic padding and liner. Textile trimmed, liner flapped over top of wall, and covered by coping

Outer wall

Inner wall built on base slab

Concrete ring footing for the wall, 6 inches thick (on 6 inches hardpan)

Concrete base slab, 4–6 inches thick, poured onto liner

↗ A rectangular tank pond with the liner both completely hidden and protected by the base slab and the cavity walls.

Circular sunken pond surrounded by paving

2–4 inches gravel and 2–4 inches sand spread under the cut paving

Stone paving cut to top of pond edge

Synthetic padding trimmed back and liner flapped over top of wall

Brick wall built onto base slab, synthetic padding and liner behind

Concrete slab, 6 inches thick, poured on top of liner plus synthetic padding

Hole lined with synthetic padding and liner sandwich

↗ A circular tank pond with the liner running under the base slab and up between the brick wall and the soil.

Raised pond with an irregular shape

↘ A raised pond with a brick inner wall and stone outer wall. The sandwich of synthetic padding and butyl rubber liner runs under the base slab and up between the two walls.

Outer wall built from stone with a slab coping

Inner wall built from bricks with the liner flapped over the top

Synthetic padding and liner sandwich spread over the site

Concrete ring footing, 5¼ inches thick, to define the shape of the pond

For how to build a raised pond (regular shape) with a flexible liner, see page 29.

EDGE TREATMENTS

The primary function of an edging is to secure and conceal the top edge of the liner. The method will depend on the design of the pond. For a wildlife pond, it can simply be covered with soil. Raised ponds require a wall at least 10 inches wide. The edging is laid on a generous bed of mortar, after trimming the synthetic padding away from the flap of liner (see pages 36–37).

PIPEWORK

The pipework must all be planned out at the very start of the project. The best option is to run the pipes over the rim of the pond (see pages 20–21).

Raised ponds

How do I design and build a raised pond?

If you want to build an attractive, low-maintenance, self-contained pond, but avoid digging a hole, a raised pond is the answer. There are three easy ways to proceed. You can set a preformed liner on a concrete slab and ring it with a brick or stone wall; you can build a rectilinear ring wall and line it with flexible butyl rubber sheeting; or you can build a rectilinear or circular ring wall and coat the inside with well tamped and sculpted concrete.

ADVANTAGES AND DISADVANTAGES

Advantages of raised ponds

- ✔ No heavy, deep digging.
- ✔ General maintenance can be done with the minimum of bending—a real plus point for older people.
- ✔ Fish and plants can be viewed from a comfortable sitting position.
- ✔ Safer than sunken ponds if there are young children in the family.

Disadvantages of raised ponds

- ✘ They can occasionally look out of place in some gardens.
- ✘ Really small raised ponds can freeze over in winter and overheat in the summer, killing fish.
- ✘ Brick walls need to be two bricks thick so that the coping bricks or tiles can be firmly bedded in place.

Container ponds

These are containers that can be moved when they are empty. (See page 66.)

Wooden half-barrel ~ If you opt for one of these, make sure that the metal hoops are held in place with nails and leave the inside untreated, so that the wooden staves can expand to form a watertight fit. Avoid imitation barrels.

Ceramic pot ~ A well glazed pot that is wider at the rim than at the base.

HOW TO BUILD A RAISED POND WITH A PREFORMED LINER

↑ → A preformed liner is put in position on a concrete slab and a brick ring wall built around it. The lip of the liner rests on the wall. The space between the inner wall and the liner is packed with sand to give additional support to the liner's molded shelf, which is for aquatic plants.

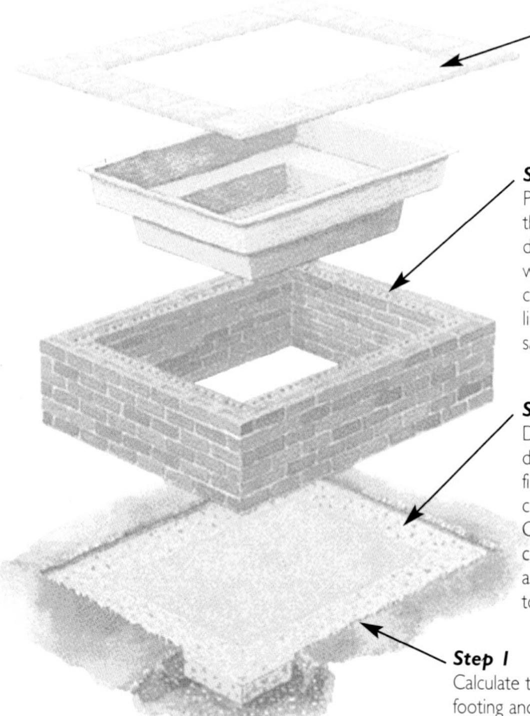

Step 4
Spread mortar on top of the walls and bed the coping tiles in place.

Step 3
Position the liner on the slab and build a double-thickness brick wall around it, filling the cavity between the liner and the wall with sand as you go.

Step 2
Dig the footing to a depth of 12 inches, and fill it with 6 inches of compacted hardpan. Cover with 6 inches of concrete. (The central area will contain sand to support the liner.)

Step 1
Calculate the size of the footing and mark it on the ground with pegs and string.

HOW TO BUILD A RAISED POND WITH A FLEXIBLE LINER

Step 2 →
Lay the butyl rubber across the footing and build the cavity wall. (The butyl rubber is sandwiched between the two walls, and the top edge is trapped under the coping tiles.)

Step 5
Cut the coping tiles to fit, so that they bridge the two walls and trap the liner, and bed them on mortar.

Step 4
Where the liner exits the cavity wall, cut away the protective textile to reveal the butyl rubber. Fold it toward the pond and trim flush with the edge of the wall.

Step 1
Dig a 12-inch-deep footing, then fill it half with hardpan and half with concrete.

Step 3
Spread 2 inches of concrete over the liner.

↗ → A raised pond can be built to any shape you wish by constructing a brick cavity ring wall on a concrete slab, with a flexible butyl rubber liner laid across the base (and then running up between the cavity walls). A thin layer of concrete is spread over the base to protect the liner.

HOW TO BUILD A ROUND RAISED POND WITH A FOUNTAIN

↘ Dig out an octagonal footing. Leaving a 12-inch-square sump hole in the center, fill it with concrete. Build a circular wall 24 inches high. Lay the butyl rubber liner to flop inside the sump hole, across the concrete, and up the wall. Insert the sump, pump, and pipes. Render the inside of the pond with tamped concrete, sculpting it with a flat trammel turned from a central axis. Bed the coping bricks in mortar, trapping the butyl rubber.

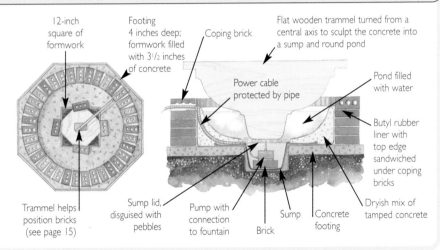

12-inch square of formwork

Footing 4 inches deep; formwork filled with 3 1/2 inches of concrete

Coping brick

Flat wooden trammel turned from a central axis to sculpt the concrete into a sump and round pond

Power cable protected by pipe

Pond filled with water

Butyl rubber liner with top edge sandwiched under coping bricks

Trammel helps position bricks (see page 15)

Sump lid, disguised with pebbles

Pump with connection to fountain

Brick

Sump

Concrete footing

Dryish mix of tamped concrete

MORE RAISED POND DESIGNS

The butyl rubber liner is supported on the stepped inner wall, to make a planting shelf.

Built with rendered concrete blocks, the outer surface is decorated with tile mosaic.

Half the depth of butyl rubber liner is supported in the hole, with soil banked on the ground.

A brick ring wall is built up around a preformed liner and decorated with pebbles.

Split-level waterways

Is it hard to build a split-level waterway?

Split-level waterways, canals, ponds, and rills are wonderful fun, both to build and to see in action. They do involve a lot of hard work and can be tricky to construct, especially if you are building the item on a flat site; however, the end results are amazing and well worth the effort. If you enjoy watching moving water, you will love gazing at these large sheets and ribbons of water sliding, folding, trickling, and rippling in the sunlight.

THE OPTIONS

A split-level waterway is characterized by having a header pool or tank and a reservoir pool or tank. Water is pumped from the reservoir up the header pool, where it brims over and runs down into the reservoir pool, and the cycle begins again. The exciting part is the way the water brims over.

For example, the water might rush through a narrow spillway, flow gently over a wide spillway, or fall quietly into a long canal. The way the water falls depends on the power of the pump, the size and shape of the two pools, the slope of the garden, the height of the drop, the width of the spillway, and the length of run between the two pools. Do you want lots of splashing, in which case you need a narrow spillway and a long drop, or do you want the quiet calm of a canal?

Suitable locations

The water needs to drop from one level to another. If you do not have a sloping garden, you will have to create a drop.

Sloping garden ~ The natural slope of the ground gives you the easy option of building the tanks in a stepped formation, allowing the creation of linked pools at different levels.

Patio drop ~ If the site is almost level, you can position a very deep header tank on a built-up patio, so that the water can drop the height of the tank.

Canal drop ~ If the site is absolutely flat, the header tank can be at ground level, while the reservoir can be in the form of an excavated sump. This is a good option for a long canal.

SPLIT-LEVEL CONSTRUCTIONS

Canal with underground sump

➜ The canal relies not so much on a slope, but rather on a pump pushing water along its length. With this example, the header tank is made by creating a step, one brick high, at one end of the canal, while the reservoir is formed by digging a hole at the other. The water is pumped from the reservoir to the header tank.

Linked ponds

↗ If you want to increase the impact of an existing pond, linked ponds are a good option. All you do is build the second pond hard up against the first, so that there is a step down from one pond to another. The second pond can be built either higher or lower than the first, but this will depend on the shape and character of your site.

Raised patio pond with spillway step

↗ The raised patio split-level pond looks especially good alongside the house. Water is pumped up to the header pool, where it brims over through a narrow spillway to give a very vigorous flow. The flow is made all the more dynamic and convincing by having the spill tile (the point where the water flows over) adjusted so that there is a generous overhang. This design is very well thought through—the edge of the header pool is flush with the patio, and the three steps fit nicely into the total height.

HOW TO BUILD A SPLIT-LEVEL POND

A split-level pond made from two brick pools set side by side, with a break in the adjoining walls so that the water brims and flows from one pool to the other. The height of the water drop has been governed by the desire to have the edge of the upper pool flush with the patio.

Step 6
Build a narrow spillway by leaving out one or two bricks and inserting a jutting spill tile to create a generous lip.

Step 5
Top the walls with a course of soldier bricks (bricks set on edge).

Concrete blocks are cheaper than bricks. One block can be used instead of six bricks.

Cavity wall made of bricks plus concrete blocks

Spill tile directs water flow

Butyl rubber liner

Concrete, 2³/₄–4 inches thick

Concrete, 8 inches thick

Step 4
Lay a thin layer of concrete over the base of the tanks, so that the butyl rubber liner is protected from damage.

Step 1
Dig the footing for the reservoir pool 16–20 inches deep, depending on the site. It should extend 6 inches away from each wall. Fill with 4 inches of compacted hardpan and top with 8 inches of concrete.

Step 2
Set the footing for the upper (header) pool higher, so that the difference in levels equals one concrete block plus two bricks. Make the footing as in Step 1.

Step 3
Build the two tanks to share the adjoining wall. Note how the butyl rubber liner runs across the footing slab and up through the cavity wall. Build the wall to a height to suit the slope of the site. Leave space for the spillway.

RILLS

A rill is best defined as a gully of water that by its very design looks as if it belongs to an industrial or rural water-moving scheme. Rills give the impression that they have a function—for example, a source of water for a millpond. A rill is all on one level, and looks like a much narrower version of a canal, with one or both ends hidden from view. If you build a long gully with a header pool at one end and a reservoir on the other, you have a rill.

How to build a rill flush with the ground

Step 4
Render the inside of the rill with a 1¹/₄-inch layer of cement-rich mortar.

Step 5
Top the walls with a course of soldier bricks (bricks set on edge).

Step 6
Build the reservoir and header pools to suit, with the pump in the reservoir pool and the pipes and cables buried alongside the rill.

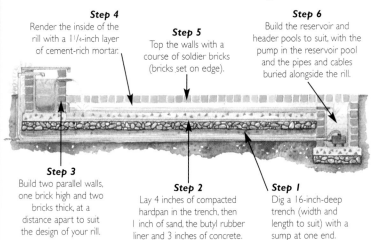

Step 3
Build two parallel walls, one brick high and two bricks thick, at a distance apart to suit the design of your rill.

Step 2
Lay 4 inches of compacted hardpan in the trench, then 1 inch of sand, the butyl rubber liner and 3 inches of concrete.

Step 1
Dig a 16-inch-deep trench (width and length to suit) with a sump at one end.

MORE THOUGHTS

In the sense that a rill is no more than a gully that looks as though it has an architectural, industrial, or rural past, it could be made from just about anything—brick, concrete, stone, ceramic, plastic, glass, metal, or sawn wood. The key words associated with a rill are "architectural" and "structured." Rills tend to be geometrical in design, with lots of straight lines and right-angled corners. The depth of water you can have is governed by the size of the pump in relation to the length, depth, and width of the gully.

Quick alternatives

If you want to build a swift rill across an area of woodland, you could edge it with railroad ties and cover the butyl rubber with a layer of dry bricks.

You could look for an industrial gully—plastic, ceramic, or metal—and use it so that it is on view.

You could build the whole rill from dry bricks or blocks bedded in sand, hiding the butyl rubber under the structure.

Wildlife ponds

Can I build a wildlife pond in my small garden?

Even the most compact of gardens can host a wildlife pond—it you leave a bucket of water in the garden for a month, it will turn green with algae and you'll find gnat larvae and snails. If you leave it for six months, birds, frogs, mice, and lizards will be attracted to feed there. In both a mini pond like this and a larger version, an ever-changing cast of characters will develop—a place where water, wildlife. and plants come together to create an entrancing ecosystem.

A peaceful pond with a beach and bank on one side, and an area of planting on the other. It is home to a wide range of animals. When deciding on the scale of a wildlife pond, it is preferable to opt for the biggest pond that the space will allow.

WILDLIFE POND TROUBLESHOOTING

A successful wildlife pond needs to be perfectly balanced, with just the right amount of planting, good-quality water, not too many of any single species, no exotic fish, and so on. Only experience will tell you if the balance is right.

If you notice that the water is green, there is an overgrowth of algae. Maybe there is not enough wildlife to feed on it, or too few or too many fish. Ideally, the water needs to be clear and bright, with no bubbles or scum. Reduce light levels and encourage frogs and other creatures. Generally, it takes at least a season for the lifecycle of the pond to settle down. Make only small changes, leaving plenty of time in between.

HOW TO BUILD A WILDLIFE POND

It is best to build wildlife ponds using a flexible butyl rubber liner. Dig out the hole and put down a ring footing for a retaining wall around what will be the edge of the pond, then spread out the synthetic padding and butyl rubber. Build a wall (two or three bricks high) on the footing, then flap the liner up and over the wall. Finally, cover the wall and planting shelves with soil.

Although the basic design is simple enough, it is the detail—the extent, depth, and width of the planting shelves, and the height of the wall—that help to shape the character of the pond. So if, for example, you want a heavy border of marginal plants to surround the pond, you need to build a planting shelf all the way around it. If you want marginal plants on one half and a deep fall-away straight into the water on the other, you would have the planting shelf running only halfway around the pond, and so on.

Step 6
Trim back the synthetic padding and fold in the butyl rubber over the top of the wall. Cover the wall and the planting shelf with soil.

Step 5
Build a two-brick-high wall on the ring footing at the edge of the pond. Lay a row of dry bricks along the edge of the planting shelf.

Step 4
Cover the edge of the butyl rubber with another layer of synthetic padding to extend right down to the edge of the planting shelf.

Step 3
Cover the site with synthetic padding, followed by the butyl rubber liner.

Step 2
Dig a trench, 8 inches wide and 8 inches deep, around the edge of the pond, and fill with 6 inches of concrete.

Step 1
Dig out the hole and sculpt the soil to include the planting shelf and a 3-in-1 slope (see page 13) down from the edge of the shelf.

LIFECYCLE OF A WILDLIFE POND

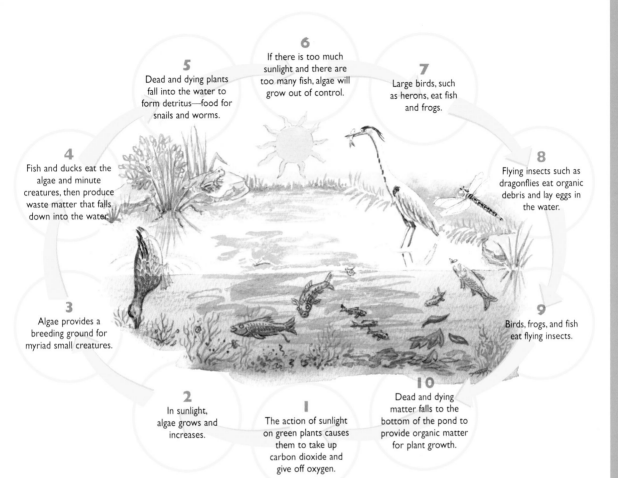

6
If there is too much sunlight and there are too many fish, algae will grow out of control.

5
Dead and dying plants fall into the water to form detritus—food for snails and worms.

7
Large birds, such as herons, eat fish and frogs.

4
Fish and ducks eat the algae and minute creatures, then produce waste matter that falls down into the water.

8
Flying insects such as dragonflies eat organic debris and lay eggs in the water.

3
Algae provides a breeding ground for myriad small creatures.

9
Birds, frogs, and fish eat flying insects.

2
In sunlight, algae grows and increases.

1
The action of sunlight on green plants causes them to take up carbon dioxide and give off oxygen.

10
Dead and dying matter falls to the bottom of the pond to provide organic matter for plant growth.

MAINTAINING AN ECOSYSTEM

An ecosystem is the interaction between living things and their environment. For a successful wildlife pond, a balance must be found between your preferences (for flowers and lots of fish, for example) and the requirements of the ecosystem. If you introduce too many fish, they will eat too many small creatures, causing the algae to grow out of control. Don't be in too much of a hurry to top up the pond with water from your domestic supply, because it contains minerals and salts that encourage the growth of algae.

Water-lilies give shade, and shade inhibits the growth of algae.

Try to be tolerant. If you want birds, you need gnats. If you like fish, you have to settle for a soupy mix of green water and crustaceans.

Thin out plants and remove any that are dying, but apart from that, if the pond looks fine, leave it alone.

Wildlife ponds are a haven for dragonflies.

CHECKING WATER QUALITY

If fish look unhealthy and plants out of condition, the chances are that the water is out of balance, with too many nitrates and salts. Check the pH level using a testing kit (it should be below 8.5). Clear away decomposing plants and make sure that highly alkaline water isn't leaching into the pond.

If normally shy fish change their behavior and can be seen rolling around on the surface and pushing each other, don't assume that they are stressed. It could be the mating season.

A surfeit of algae, together with dead fish, indicate that the water is polluted or the oxygen level too low. Clear the waste matter, introduce more oxygenating plants, and add rainwater.

Tiled and mosaic ponds

Would a tiled or mosaic pond suit my courtyard?

Tiles let you inject color and pattern into the creation of a pond, whether as an unusual surround, or as a fascinating design glinting beneath the surface of the water. Mosaic gives you scope to paint a picture—from a simple underwater scene to a copy of Botticelli's *Venus*—it's all down to your imagination. The added interest of a mosaic design provides an attractive focus for a small area and is ideal for an inner-city courtyard garden.

Reconstituted stone imitation terra-cotta tiles add warm blocks of color, and tone with the brickwork of this raised pool.

The outside face of a raised pool with salvaged Victorian Delft tiles set in the brickwork—a good choice for a patio or courtyard.

A mosaic made from broken ceramic tiles fitted on a dish-shaped raised pond. Cobblestones hide the pump.

TILE PATTERNS

If you enjoy color and pattern and want to build a decorative pool with the minimum of effort, you cannot do better than a bold tile design. Tiles are waterproof and the design possibilities are extensive.

Four-by-four random square color

Stepped Art Deco classic

Checkerboard with patterned infill

Horizontal bold color stripe

Diamond diagonal counterchange

MOSAIC PATTERNS

If you enjoy working in miniature and want to build a decorative pool with a complex design, mosaics are a good choice. You can opt for using purpose-made glass mosaic, broken ceramic tiles, or broken ceramic ware.

Leaping fish

Fantasy frog

Stylized sunflower

Japanese waves

A study in blue

SUITABLE SITUATIONS

Shallow, clear-water pools are ideal candidates. Use waterproof adhesives and grout, so that the designs are both weatherproof and waterproof, and can be applied to the outside or inside of a pool.

HOW TO STICK DOWN THE TILES

Tiles and mosaics need a firm base of either bricks or blocks. Brush the area to remove loose debris and render it with a cement-rich mortar, making it as smooth and level as possible.

Draw the design on tracing paper and transfer it to the surface to be decorated. Turn complex motifs into cardboard templates that can be used as a guide. With the tracing set flat on a board, fill each area with pieces of tile or mosaic cut to fit. When you are happy with it, spread adhesive on the wall, a small area at a time, and stick the tiles in place. Leave to dry, then fill the joints with waterproof grout and wipe clean with a damp cloth.

Quick ponds

If you are keen, it is easily possible to build a pond on a weekend by choosing one of the simpler methods of construction. A preformed liner is a good option when you lack time. If you are short of money, you can pare your costs by using a reclaimed tank or some heavy-duty plastic sheeting. If you want to build a large, impressive pond and don't mind a bit of heavy lifting, a pond made of railroad ties will fit the bill. There are lots of exciting possibilities!

I am short of time—can I build a pond on a weekend?

CONTAINERS

Containers make very nice ponds. If something holds water, it can be turned into a pond—from ceramic flowerpots to half-barrels and dustbins.

One quick option, which instantly adds a new dimension to the garden, is to gather lots of different ceramic pots—various sizes, shapes, and colors—and group them at different levels. Once these are filled with water and plants, the area instantly becomes a pondlike environment that attracts wildlife.

WOODEN PATIO PONDS

An easy-to-build patio pond comprising a fountain covered by a quirky pointed roof.

A patio pond can be as basic as a sheet of pre-cut butyl rubber together with synthetic padding, through to a barrel pond made from preformed fiberglass. Some designs involve digging, while others can simply be put together in a few hours, then filled with water and switched on. If you don't want to have to dig, then an easy-to-build wooden design like this is a good option.

RECLAIMED WATERTIGHT OBJECTS

It is possible to make a pond from any suitable reclaimed container. You could use a decorative water tank set above ground, an industrial container, a cattle trough, a farm cistern, and so on. We have seen a very nice little pond made out of a plastic chemical container, about 3 feet square and half buried in the ground. Another garden boasts a huge pond made from a reclaimed stainless-steel milk storage tank, about 12 feet long, of the type that dairy farmers use.

Once you spot a likely candidate, you need to consider the implications. Is it really a good idea? How can it be transported? Can it be lifted? Will it go through the gate? Can you clean off any residues to make it safe for pond flora and fauna?

HOW TO MAKE A RAILROAD TIE POND

You need twelve railroad ties, a sheet of PVC, old underfelt, and a wheelbarrow-load of fine gravel. Dig out a hole deep enough to take three tie squares set one on top of another. Position two tie squares in the ground and cover them with the felt, followed by the plastic. Fill the pond with water. Sit the other four ties in a square that holds the plastic in place. Finally, put a layer of gravel in the bottom of the pond to protect the plastic.

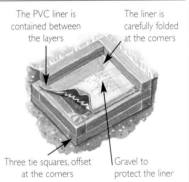

The PVC liner is contained between the layers

The liner is carefully folded at the corners

Three tie squares, offset at the corners

Gravel to protect the liner

HOW TO MAKE A ROCKPOOL

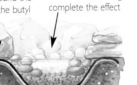

Rocks around the edge of the butyl

Cobblestones and gravel complete the effect

A shallow, sculpted hole

Synthetic padding covered by butyl rubber

Ponds inspired by seaside and riverside rockpools can be exciting and dynamic, and are perfect if you want to build a pond on a weekend. You need a sheet of butyl rubber with a sheet of synthetic padding to match (size to suit your needs), a good number of large feature rocks, plus cobblestones and fine gravel. Dig out the hole, line it with the synthetic padding and butyl rubber, and then spend time carefully arranging the rocks and gravel for best effect.

Pond edgings

Can I get away without building an edging?

Pond edgings are very important. Although they are not always visible, they hold a structure together and set the mood and character of a pond. Whatever your choice of edging—soil, stones, brickwork, wood, turf, or shingle— it is vital that it is long-lasting and stable (this does not necessarily involve using concrete and mortar). The edging needs to be carefully planned to ensure that the end result suits both the style of the pond and existing garden features.

NATURAL-LOOKING EDGINGS FOR SUNKEN PONDS

The trick with a natural pond is to construct the edging so that all traces of the liner are hidden from view. Suitable options for edging a natural pond include a dense planting of bog and marginal plants, large rocks or boulders, layered stone, a beach, or a combination of these.

If you want the pond to look like a forest pool, you should go for dense planting; if you want a seaside or riverside rockpool, you should use weathered stone; if you want a meandering stream effect, you should use a mixture of layered rock and planting.

All edgings, of whatever type, require a good footing— either a concrete slab or a kerb. For example, with the planted edge, you cannot see anything other than plants and soil surrounding the pond, but hidden below the soil is a concrete ring footing supporting a low wall, tucked away so that it doesn't spoil the illusion.

In this pond, soil and plants cover an edging of concrete and brick, creating the illusion of a natural pond.

Rockpool boulder edging

❧ *Each boulder is set on a pad of concrete, and tilted so that its weight is thrown backward. The liner runs under and up behind the boulders, so that they are partially underwater.*

❧ *A pond built with a butyl rubber liner and a concrete ring footing supporting a brick wall. The slope is covered with cobblestones and shingle, topped with soil. The water comes halfway up the beach.*

Beachside edging

Meandering stream edging

❧ *Carefully selected slabs of stone are set on a pad of concrete to create a striated dry-stone wall that tilts back against the soil. The liner runs up between the wall and the soil bank.*

❧ *A mixture of bog planting and stone. The pond is built with a flexible butyl rubber liner, ring footing and brick wall to secure and define the edge. The soil and stones are arranged to conceal the brick wall.*

Bog garden rocky edging

FORMAL EDGINGS FOR SUNKEN PONDS

A formal pond edged with reconstituted slabs, set in the middle of a patio.

↑ A formal edging is defined as being an edging that isn't built in imitation of nature. It might consist of anything from paving, brick, or stone through to reconstituted stone, concrete, wood, or metal; however, most formal ponds are edged with stone or brick in classical architectural tradition.

Brick on edge

Brick paving patio with a course of soldier bricks (on-edge bricks) for the edging.

Reconstituted stone

A delightful octagonal pond set amid reconstituted stone paving.

Railroad tie

A square pond with an edging made from railroad ties backed with bricks.

Cleft-stone paving

A long, formal, semisunken pond with a surround of cleft-stone paving.

Curb and cobblestones

A cast concrete kerb edging with a surround of egg-size cobblestones set in mortar.

Concrete and mosaic

A circular pond with a cast concrete edging, detailed with a mosaic infill.

EDGINGS FOR RAISED PONDS

The retaining wall for a raised pond is very much in evidence, so the capping chosen to top it is clearly seen. The width of the wall in relation to the coping must be carefully considered.

Many people build a wall that is only one brick thick and flap the butyl rubber liner over it (or sit the preformed liner in place), and then paste mortar on top of the wall and bed the coping in position. However, the narrowness of the wall means that the coping soon falls off. The solution is a two-brick-thick wall to provide plenty of surface contact between the wall and the coping.

Roof tile sandwich

A traditional coping made from a double course of plain roof tiles.

Soldier bricks

Bricks set on edge are the perfect solution for a simple, round pond.

Cut stone

A double row of cut stone slices gives a generous finish to this round pond.

Reconstituted stone

A traditional wall with a paver coping—all made from reconstituted stone.

Slate cladding

Built from concrete blocks, this raised pond is completely clad in slate.

Log roll

Log-roll edging around a preformed raised pond, topped with soil and plants.

PIPEWORK AND EDGE PROBLEMS

Pipes must be installed without damaging the integrity of the liner. It is best never to make a hole in the liner (even if some manufacturers advise otherwise), but to simply run pipes over the edge of the liner and hide them under foliage (see pages 20–21).

SURROUNDING AREA

Although a formal pond can provide a beautiful contrast in a wild garden, it is more usual to set one amid an area of paving or in a well-tended lawn, so that it can be approached and seen in comfort. Most formal ponds are part of a larger scheme or grand design, and the surrounding area needs to be considered right at the start of the project (see pages 22–23).

PROPS

Formal ponds and their surrounds tend to be inspired by geometry—circles, squares, and hexagons—with straight approaches leading the eye to the pond. These go hand in hand with formal props such as classical statues, large pots, low stone or brick walls, and trees arranged in neat lines. As part of your research, visit parks and grand historic mansions to see stylistic possibilities.

Pond plants

How many groups of water plants are there?

If we list the plants according to their position in the pond, there are five main groups: deep-water plants, submerged plants, floating plants, marginal plants, and bog garden plants. Some specialists pull water-lilies out of the deep-water group to create a sixth group (and likewise make a seventh group for lotuses), but it is simpler to stick with the five-group classification—it is clear and logical, and it tells you all you need to know about what type of plant goes where.

A natural pond with a boggy area planted with irises and reeds to create background interest. Submerged oxygenators around the margins keep the water clear, and a large raft of water-lilies supplies color, helps stop the water becoming murky, and provides cover.

STYLE, SCALE, AND OTHER CONSIDERATIONS

Think of a pond in much the same way as a flower border—as something that needs background foliage and swathes of color to enhance it.

Start by getting one or two special feature plants for color and drama—for example, a water-lily for water cover, and a lotus for flower height. Before purchasing, read the label carefully, and try to picture how the mature plant will relate to the overall character of the pond. Will it become too big and dominate the area? Would it be better to go for a smaller variety?

Once you have decided on the feature plants, choose the submerged and floating plants. Submerged plants are particularly useful if you want fish, because they provide food and a habitat. It is vital to buy plants to suit the diameter and depth of your pond, because many will die if they are planted in water that is the incorrect depth for them. Plant from spring through to late summer.

POND PLANT GROUPS

The five plant groups furnish plants for each area of the pond. Working from the sides of the pond through to the depths, you need bog plants for the pond surrounds (these will also supply cover for animals) and marginals, which have submerged roots and leaves and flowers above the surface, for the shallow water at the edges. Submerged plants oxygenate the water, floating plants provide surface cover, and deep-water plants, with submerged roots and leaves and flowers above the surface, help keep the water clear and cool and provide cover for fish.

GENERAL PLANTING NOTES

Plan the project so that you can start planting out between spring and late summer. If cement has been used in the pond's construction, the pond will need to be filled and drained several times over a two-week period and, finally, the water left to stand for a week before planting.

Bog plants ~ Many bog plants thrive in really wet soil, but others like it moist rather than waterlogged. Irises can simply be divided and heeled in.

Marginals ~ The recommended depth for marginals ranges, according to variety, from a position just below the surface, to 6 1/2 inches deep. The depth of water is critical. Measure the depth of water and buy container-grown plants to plant in baskets.

Floating plants ~ To plant, these are just dropped into the water. In the late fall, the foliage will break away and the seed pods will sink to the bottom.

Submerged oxygenators ~ Sold in bunches, these are best divided and planted out in baskets (so that you can control rampant growers). Plant several varieties.

Deep-water plants ~ This group contains water-lilies, lotuses, and vast numbers of other plants with floating leaves, which flourish in depths ranging from 10–36 inches. Taking into account the future spread of other plants, the deep-water plants should cover no more than half the water's surface.

POND PLANT GROUPS

Submerged plants
(see page 42)

Submerged plants, also called oxygenators, grow up from the bottom of the pond, and their foliage sometimes, but not always, breaks the surface of the water. The foliage gives off bubbles of oxygen and the roots use up waste nutrients in the water. They are good if you want to encourage fish.

Floating plants
(see page 41)

Floating plants do, as their name suggests, float on the surface of the water, with their fine roots hanging down like a curtain. The roots form cover for spawning fish, and the foliage also provides a habitat for aquatic insects.

Marginal plants
(see page 43)

Marginals are primarily ornamental, giving lots of color and interest, but they also supply shelter from wind and rain, a habitat for emerging dragonflies, and cover for fish and frogs. In the context of a formal pond, marginals beautifully blur the boundary between the sides of the pond and the water.

Bog plants
(see page 54)

In a wildlife pond, bog plants not only provide cover for frogs and insects, but help blend the pond into the garden.

Deep-water plants
(see page 40)

You need to cover about half of the surface of the pond with the floating leaves of deep-water plants. The leaves give shade to fish and help to keep the water clear by reducing algae growth. With their roots growing in the bottom of the pond, these plants help to clear up excess nutrients and fish waste.

SOME USEFUL PLANTING SCHEMES

SCHEME	DEEP WATER	SUBMERGED	FLOATING	MARGINAL	BOG
A natural-looking wildlife pond with a large bog garden, a wide range of marginals, native wildlife, fish, frogs, and newts.	Cow-lily (*Nuphar*), Cape pond weed (*Aponogeton distachyos*), Floating heart (*Nymphoides peltata*)	Water buttercup (*Ranunculus aquatilis*), Curled pondweed (*Potamogeton crispus*), Hornwort (*Ceratophyllum demersum*)	Chile parrotfeather (*Myriophyllum aquaticum*), Azolla (*Azolla caroliniana*)	Blue flag (*Iris versicolor*), Sweet grass (*Glyceria maxima*), Waterarum (*Calla palustris*), Sweet flag (*Acorus calamus*)	Eulalia grass (*Miscanthus sinensis* "Zebrinus"), Royal fern (*Osmunda regalis*), White false hellebore (*Veratrum album*), Speedwell (*Veronica beccabunga*)
A formal pond with a stone surround and a fountain at the center. **A large pond.**	Japanese cow-lily (*Nuphar japonica*), Cape water-lily (*Nymphaea capensis*)	Common bladderwort (*Utricularia vulgaris*), Hornwort (*Ceratophyllum demersum*), Curled pond weed (*Potamogeton crispus*)	Water soldier (*Stratiotes aloides*)	Not applicable	Not applicable
A raised patio pond with a very small fountain and goldfish.	Aurora water-lily (*Nymphaea* "Aurora")	Canadian waterweed (*Elodea canadensis*), Willow moss (*Fontinalis antipyretica*)	Frogbit (*Hydrocharis morsus-ranae*)	Marsh marigold (*Caltha palustris*)	Not applicable

Deep-water plants

My pond isn't deep. Can I have deep-water plants?

Deep-water plants are essential to the overall well-being of a pond. The floating leaves provide cover for fish and inhibit the growth of algae by blocking off some sunlight, while the roots dissolve and absorb nutrients and fish waste. If your pond is at least 12 inches deep, it will provide a suitable home.

Water-lilies are a popular deep-water plant, and look stunning en masse.

SOME COMMON DEEP-WATER PLANTS

Japanese cow-lily

Nuphar japonica

Characteristics ~ A beautiful deciduous perennial, with erect, brilliant yellow flowers and floating heart-shaped leaves. Grows in water to a depth of about 12 inches and has a spread of up to 3 feet.

Special note ~ Prefers still or slow-moving water and lots of sunshine. Can be divided in the spring.

Cape pondweed

Aponogeton distachyos

Characteristics ~ A delicate, almost evergreen perennial, with heavily scented white flowers. Grows in water to a depth of 24 inches and has a spread of 4 feet.

Special note ~ Prefers slow-moving water, lots of sunshine, and mild winters. Can be propagated by seed or by division in spring.

Cape water-lily

Nymphaea capensis

Characteristics ~ A beautiful water-lily with large, blue, star-shaped flowers and big, wavy-edged leaves. Grows in water to a depth of 12–24 inches and has a spread of 8 feet.

Special note ~ If the conditions are right, this water-lily will completely cover a small pond. It likes a hot summer and a mild winter.

Floating heart

Nymphoides peltata

Characteristics ~ Pretty yellow star-like flowers, small heart-shaped leaves. A deciduous perennial, which grows in water to a depth of 18 inches and has a spread of up to 24 inches.

Special note ~ A semihardy plant, which likes lots of sun and will flower throughout the summer. It can be propagated by division in spring.

European white water-lily

Nymphaea alba

Characteristics ~ A vigorous, prolific flowerer with creamy-white double flowers and round, dark green leaves. Grows in water to a depth of 36 inches and has a spread of 7 feet.

Special note ~ One of the few water-lilies that will tolerate cold water. A good choice for a large wildlife pond.

OTHER PLANTS

There are hundreds of different water plants that are defined as being suitable for deep water. Their primary function is to provide cover and shade, and many of them are chosen more for the size and character of their leaves than their flowers. Bear this in mind when making your selection.

SPECIAL NOTES

If you have a large, very shallow pool, you can omit deep-water plants and use broad-leaved floaters to supply cover and shade. If you want a really stunning plant, you could try the Amazon water-lily (*Nymphaea* "Victoria Amazonica"). The flowers last only a couple of days, but the leaves grow up to 8 feet across and look rather like round trays with upturned rims.

Floating plants

These plants have submerged roots, and leaves that float on the surface or just below it. Some are rooted at the bottom of the pond; others have floating roots. Floating plants produce swift cover, which is useful when a pond is new, but some tend to be invasive and need to be controlled with great care.

Floating plants must be carefully monitored to ensure they don't take over the pond.

What is the definition of a floating plant?

SOME COMMON FLOATING PLANTS

Chile parrotfeather
Myriophyllum aquaticum

Characteristics ~ A fast-growing, deciduous, perennial plant that grows as a spreading underwater carpet. The roots can take hold in the bottom of a shallow, muddy pond.

Special note ~ An invasive plant—it can soon crowd out everything else in the pond. Check that it isn't prohibited.

Salvinia
Salvinia auriculata

Characteristics ~ A free-floating perennial fern, with green to purple leaves, which is delicate and exotic. The spreading colonies can be invasive.

Special note ~ The branched stems can grow up to 1¼ inches in height. A bad (possibly illegal) choice if the pond is linked to a natural watercourse. Check that it isn't prohibited.

Azolla
Azolla caroliniana

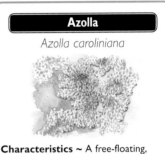

Characteristics ~ A free-floating, fast-growing perennial with small white flowers and rosettes of small, kidney-shaped leaves. Can be invasive.

Special note ~ Good for a swift, temporary covering on a new pond. A bad choice for a large pond that is part of a natural watercourse. Check that it isn't prohibited.

Water soldier
Stratiotes aloides

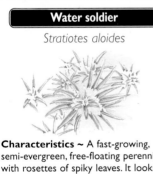

Characteristics ~ A fast-growing, semi-evergreen, free-floating perennial with rosettes of spiky leaves. It looks like a green pineapple. Semihardy.

Special note ~ This plant is unusual in that it sometimes sinks to the bottom of the pond, even in summer. New plants form as stems. Check that it isn't prohibited.

Water lettuce
Pistia stratiotes

Characteristics ~ A fast-growing, free-floating plant with spongy green leaves that cluster in a rosette shape. Not hardy in cold climates.

Special note ~ While this plant will provide swift cover, it can become invasive and crowd out everything else in the pond. Check that it isn't prohibited.

OTHER PLANTS

Floating plants are vital to the well-being of a pond, but they can grow completely out of control. You need to choose them with care. For example, while common duckweed (*Lemna minor*) runs riot, there is a slow-growing variety called *Lemna trisulca*, which can be controlled more easily.

SPECIAL NOTES

A massive overgrowth of floating plants can even block rivers and dams. In some countries, the problem is so great that you can get into a lot of trouble if you are found in possession of certain species, or if you are caught transporting them from one state or country to another. Buy plants from a reputable specialist, who can advise you about which plants are permitted.

Submerged plants

Which plants oxygenate the water?

Submerged plants are oxygenators, which thrive underwater. Their leaves are usually submerged, but sometimes the foliage breaks the surface; roots are bedded in the mud at the bottom of the pond. Some varieties flower. These plants provide shade, absorb nutrients, and generally help to keep the water clear.

Submerged plants have a job to do—oxygenating the water and helping to keep it clear.

SOME COMMON SUBMERGED PLANTS

Water buttercup

Ranunculus aquatilis

Characteristics ~ A pretty, delicate annual or perennial, with small green leaves and white and yellow flowers. Grows in water to a depth of 32 inches and has an indefinite spread.

Special note ~ Does best in large wildlife ponds, where it can spread and root in deep mud. Can be propagated by seed or division in spring.

Curled pondweed

Potamogeton crispus

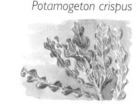

Characteristics ~ A perennial with frondlike leaves and red and white flowers that break the surface of the water. Grows in water to a depth of 3¹/₂ feet and has an indefinite spread.

Special note ~ Prefers muddy ponds that have still water and shade. Can be propagated by division or cuttings in spring.

Hornwort

Ceratophyllum demersum

Characteristics ~ A deciduous perennial, with slender, brushlike fronds and pinkish flowers. Grows in water to a depth of about 24 inches. Has an indefinite spread.

Special note ~ Good for a deep, shady, still-water pond. In spring, it can be propagated by division or by taking cuttings.

Common bladderwort

Utricularia vulgaris

Characteristics ~ A hardy, deciduous perennial, with brownish-green leaves, insect-catching bladders and yellow flowers. An unusual-looking plant, it grows in water to a depth of 4 feet. Has a spread of up to 36 inches.

Special note ~ A good choice for a wildlife pond. Can be propagated by division in spring or summer.

Willow moss

Fontinalis antipyretica

Characteristics ~ A mosslike perennial with very hairy, long, dark green slender stems and little spear-shaped leaves. Grows in water to a depth of 24 inches and has an indefinite spread.

Special note ~ A good choice for a running stream or spring. It can be propagated by division in the spring.

OTHER PLANTS

Other submerged plants include water aspidistra (*Anubias afzelii*), water violet (*Hottonia palustris*), swamp stonecrop (*Tillaea recurva*), water fern (*Ceratopteris pteridoides*), hairgrass (*Eleocharis acicularis*), and stonewort (*Chara vulgaris*). Some prefer sun and slow-moving water; others like shade and still water.

SPECIAL NOTES

Submerged oxygenators are particularly valuable in wildlife ponds and in fishponds, where they harbor insects and provide cover for fish. They are called oxygenators because they absorb carbon dioxide and give off oxygen—perfect for fish. If you look very closely at the hairier varieties, you will see lots of little bubbles of gas caught up in their fine, wavy fronds.

Marginal plants

Marginals grow in the shallows around the edge of a pond, in water 2–6 inches deep. If you can create a shelf or plateau in your pond that meets these requirements (using bricks, blocks, or soil), you can have success with a wide range of basket-grown or container-grown marginals.

Some marginals are happy to have their roots in water; others prefer a little soil.

Can a small, steep-sided pond have marginals?

SOME COMMON MARGINAL WATER PLANTS

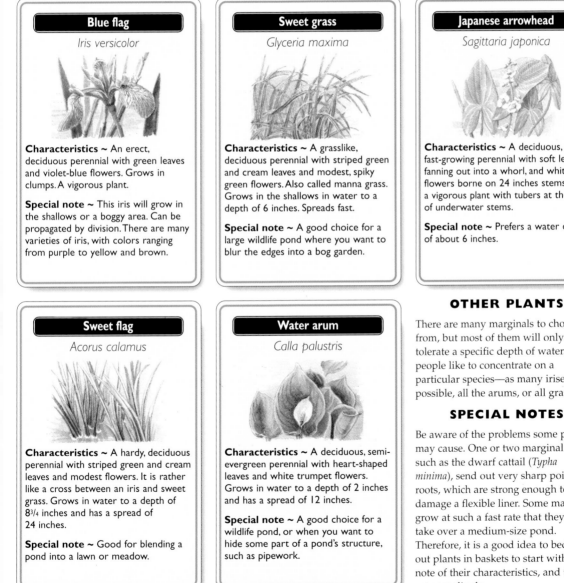

Blue flag
Iris versicolor

Characteristics ~ An erect, deciduous perennial with green leaves and violet-blue flowers. Grows in clumps. A vigorous plant.

Special note ~ This iris will grow in the shallows or a boggy area. Can be propagated by division. There are many varieties of iris, with colors ranging from purple to yellow and brown.

Sweet grass
Glyceria maxima

Characteristics ~ A grasslike, deciduous perennial with striped green and cream leaves and modest, spiky green flowers. Also called manna grass. Grows in the shallows in water to a depth of 6 inches. Spreads fast.

Special note ~ A good choice for a large wildlife pond where you want to blur the edges into a bog garden.

Japanese arrowhead
Sagittaria japonica

Characteristics ~ A deciduous, fast-growing perennial with soft leaves fanning out into a whorl, and white flowers borne on 24 inches stems. It is a vigorous plant with tubers at the end of underwater stems.

Special note ~ Prefers a water depth of about 6 inches.

Sweet flag
Acorus calamus

Characteristics ~ A hardy, deciduous perennial with striped green and cream leaves and modest flowers. It is rather like a cross between an iris and sweet grass. Grows in water to a depth of 8³/₄ inches and has a spread of 24 inches.

Special note ~ Good for blending a pond into a lawn or meadow.

Water arum
Calla palustris

Characteristics ~ A deciduous, semi-evergreen perennial with heart-shaped leaves and white trumpet flowers. Grows in water to a depth of 2 inches and has a spread of 12 inches.

Special note ~ A good choice for a wildlife pond, or when you want to hide some part of a pond's structure, such as pipework.

OTHER PLANTS

There are many marginals to choose from, but most of them will only tolerate a specific depth of water. Many people like to concentrate on a particular species—as many irises as possible, all the arums, or all grasses.

SPECIAL NOTES

Be aware of the problems some plants may cause. One or two marginal plants, such as the dwarf cattail (*Typha minima*), send out very sharp pointed roots, which are strong enough to damage a flexible liner. Some marginals grow at such a fast rate that they will take over a medium-size pond. Therefore, it is a good idea to bed out plants in baskets to start with, take note of their characteristics, and then act accordingly.

Fish

I would like to have fish and frogs—is this possible?

Size is everything when trying to establish a pond with both fish and frogs. If the pond is too small and the fish too large (in size or number), the fish will eat most of the tadpoles. The fish to pond ratio is 1 inch of fish length for every 4¼ square inches of water surface. The best way to stock a pond with fish is to do so gradually. Leave the pond for a year so that frogs, toads, and newts get established, and then introduce a small number of common goldfish.

If your main aim is to keep exhibition-grade fish, such as the giant Koi carp shown here, talk to a fish specialist before building the pond, to ensure that the planned structure will meet their needs.

NATIVE FISH

The common goldfish has been popular for about 300 years, so can now be considered as native. Along with the rudd, tench, stickleback, minnow, and carp, it is good for a cold climate where ponds are prone to icing.

STOCKING YOUR POND

Your pond will support one 1-inch-long fish for each 4½ square inches of water surface—18 small goldfish for a 43 square foot pond. If you buy fish from specialist suppliers, they will be put in a plastic bag with a small amount of air for the journey. When you get home, undo the bag and sit it in the water at the side of the pond. After an hour, gently tip the bag so that pond water runs into the bag. If all is well, the fish will quietly swim off.

TOP BUYING TIPS

Always choose your fish with care, by sticking to these guidelines.

Supplier ~ Choose a reputable specialist. Ideally, each tank in the shop should be fitted with its own filtered water supply, to avoid disease. There should be a soft net, plastic bags, and air/oxygen available. You should be able to choose your own fish.

Health ~ A healthy fish will have bright, clear eyes, an upright top fin, a straight back, and unblemished skin. Avoid fish with missing scales, a floppy top fin, or white spots on the body.

Size ~ Look for fish that are no bigger than about 3½–5¼ inches in total length. Bigger fish will not only cost a lot more, but will also have more trouble settling into a new home.

THREE COMMON TYPES OF FISH

Common goldfish

Characteristics ~ A reliable fish, good for ponds in a cold climate. Colors range from reddish-gold to creamy yellow. Grows up to 16 inches long and lives for 19–25 years.

Special note ~ Avoid fancy breeds of goldfish—they are more expensive, need more space, and are liable to perish in a cold winter.

Tench

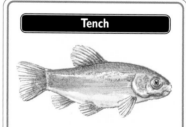

Characteristics ~ A reliable, rather shy but aggressive fish, which might well eat small fry and tadpoles. Colors range from green to a pale orange-gold. Grows up to 16 inches long and lives for 10–12 years.

Special note ~ A good idea for a large wildlife pond, but a bad idea if you want ornamental fish.

Common minnow

Characteristics ~ A swift-swimming tiddler, good for small wildlife ponds. Colors range from pale orange to silvery red-brown. Grows up to 3½ inches long and lives for 2–5 years.

Special note ~ Shoals of minnows look wonderful in ponds and streams, and are loved by small children.

MORE FISH

Roach

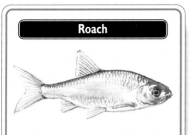

Characteristics ~ An attractive, reliable, subtly colored native fish. It is good for large, muddy-bottomed wildlife ponds and lakes. Colors range from yellow-red to brown-gold. Grows up to 10 inches long and lives for 5–8 years.

Special note ~ A fish that will tolerate both clear and muddy water.

Rudd

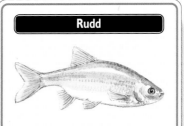

Characteristics ~ A fat-bodied fish, suitable for both small pools and large ponds. Colors range from golden yellow to orange-red. Grows up to 12 inches long and lives for 6–8 years.

Special note ~ A tough fish that will tolerate cloudy water, poor oxygen levels, and big changes in temperature.

Koi

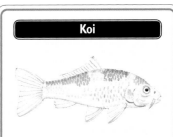

Characteristics ~ An exotic fish for both filtered ponds and large wildlife ponds. Colors range from yellow and black to white and red. Grows up to 20–36 inches long and lives for 50–100 years.

Special note ~ Koi are beautiful, but expensive and difficult to maintain. Think carefully before taking them on.

FEEDING

In an established wildlife pond, fish will live quite happily by getting most of their food from insects, plants, and detritus from the bottom of the pond. In an ornamental pond, where the bottom is clear and there is only a small range of plants, you will need to supplement their diet with good-quality pre-packed food, dried flies, ant eggs, and shredded shrimps. Feed them at midday, giving just enough to make sure that it all gets eaten and no scraps are left.

ROUTINE JOBS

Apart from giving the fish additional food, you need to work out a regular care routine. Inspect them to make sure they are healthy, with no unusual behavior or odd skin coloration. Use a net to inspect torpid fish. Check that the pond hasn't become overrun with any one type of flora or fauna, such as algae or snails. Oxygenate the water with a hose spray and generally keep an eye on the fish. Look at the pond daily to make sure that the ecosystem is running smoothly. In summer, top up the pond.

FISH TROUBLES

Fish lice
The lice are clearly visible hanging onto the body of the fish. Use a small brush dipped in paraffin to dab at and remove the lice, then dip the fish in a special fish antiseptic.

White spot
These tiny parasites look like grains of salt or sand. If you catch the disease in its early stages, you can use a proprietary cure that involves treating the fish in an isolation tank.

Fish ulcer
The disease shows itself variously as bloody spots, rotting fins, or blotchy swellings. The disease is rampant and difficult to treat, so it is best to remove and destroy the affected fish.

Fish fungus
There are several types of fungus, the most common of which are mouth fungus and cottonwool fungus. Remove affected fish and put them in an isolation tank. Small fish invariably die, but large or valuable fish can be treated with a proprietary medication. Consult a vet.

OTHER POND FAUNA

As well as teeming with microscopic life, a new pond will soon be alive with everything from frogs and newts to dragonflies and snails. Too many bugs can be a problem—they can damage the plants—but they soon (for the most part) become dinner for the other animals. If you see that there are too many of one species, either remove them or encourage animals that find them tasty prey.

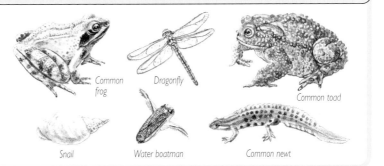

Common frog

Dragonfly

Common toad

Snail

Water boatman

Common newt

Pond maintenance

Is the maintenance very time-consuming?

If a pond has been well sited and built, and carefully stocked with healthy fish and plants, maintenance involves no more than inspecting and cleaning pumps and fountains, dividing and moving plants, occasional structural repairs, and seasonal upkeep. It is best not to wait for the various systems to clog up and grind to a halt—for example, pump breakdown, too much algae, dead fish—but rather to tackle the tasks in a logical way throughout the year.

ROUTINE JOBS

Summer tasks
Clean the filters once a week, remove algae and debris, top up with fresh water, and run the fountain on hot, muggy nights to oxygenate the water (or run a hose with a spray).

Fall care
Clean out dead leaves and debris, trim dying foliage, divide plants, remove delicate plants for overwintering indoors.

Winter jobs
Take out the last dead leaves, remove and clean pumps, filters, and fountains, put a ball in the water to break up ice.

Spring cleaning
Clean out the pond, carry out repairs, put pumps and fountains back in position, tend and replace plants.

A beautiful pond does not happen by chance, nor is it the result of a massive, once-a-year maintenance blitz. A healthy-looking pond results from a continual program of small, routine tasks.

POND MAINTENANCE TROUBLESHOOTING

PROBLEM	LIKELY CAUSE	POSSIBLE SOLUTIONS
Water level falling, fish gasping for air	Damage to the pond; not enough oxygen	• Mend the structure of the pond, repair leaks • Fit a large pump with a fountain, to oxygenate the water
Pump not working	Dirty or broken	• Clean and repair, or replace, the pump. Check the power supply
Pump works, but fountain spray is not reaching correct height	Dirty, badly set or broken	• Clean the pump so that it works to maximum efficiency • Clean the fountain and make sure that any valves are set correctly • Replace the fountain so that it is level and the head correctly adjusted
Goldfish have vanished	Herons	• Fit a low wire around the edge of the pond • Replace the goldfish with well camouflaged species, such as tench
Fish look ill	Lack of oxygen, or disease	• Inspect the fish and treat diseases. Fit a fountain. Remove scum
Green water and smelly scum	Too much sunlight	• Get lots of plants with large, floating leaves • Fit a pump and fountain • Make sure rainwater isn't flowing off a rich flowerbed
Bubbles of gas rising from bottom of pond	Too much debris at the bottom of the pond	• The pond needs completely cleaning out of all water and mud • Fit a pump and filter
Excessive plant growth	Algae	• Fit a fountain, get plants with floating leaves, be patient
Green water and lots of algae	Too many nutrients, not enough shade	• Fit a pump and fountain • Remove the algae daily • Fit a filter bed
Lots of algae and black water	Disrupted ecological balance	• Clean out the pond. Remove all water and mud, wash plants • Replant with lots of floating-leaved plants • Restock with fish

MAINTENANCE CHECKLIST

Repairing structures

Inspect all structures—bridges, decking, fences, posts, rocks, brickwork, copings, and figures—to make sure that they are in good condition. Remove or repair anything that looks dangerous. Scrub the bridge to remove buildup of slime and check the handrail. Repoint decaying brickwork. Replace cracked ceramic pots or strap them with bands of wire.

Netting

Nothing looks worse than sagging netting: either mend it or remove it, unless it is only temporary (perhaps to contain leaves). Otherwise, could you use another system? Herons can be discouraged by fine wires.

Fountains

Fountains not only look good, they also oxygenate the water—but only if they are in good working order. If the spray looks a bit feeble, clean the fountain head and check that the little valve at the bottom of the telescopic tube is set correctly. Check all the pipes and make sure that the water feed pipe isn't kinked, blocked, or cracked.

Removing excess weed

Spend time daily removing excessive plant growth with a net or stick. This is a job that children could help with, under strict supervision. Pull the strands from the water, remove and replace all the wildlife, and put the weed on the compost heap.

Adding more plants

If there is a lot of open water, you need to add more floating-leaved plants—either deep-water plants with floating leaves, or free-floating plants. This is especially important if the pond contains fish, or if algae is on the increase and the water looks cloudy.

Dividing plants

Many water plants can be propagated (also thinned out) by division. Pull floating plants apart. Iris rhizomes can be cut in half with a spade and heeled into the new position. Give unwanted plants to friends.

Pump maintenance

Turn off the power and remove the pump from the pond. Open up the pump and wash the block of filter foam. You might need to do this every week in summer, especially if the water is choked with algae.

Inspecting fish

Make a daily routine of looking at the fish. Are they feeding? Are they doing anything out of the ordinary, such as gasping for air or coming to the surface? If the fish look sluggish, to the extent that you can easily catch them with a net, make a closer inspection. Look for white spots and blotches, and damaged scales and fins. Remove suspect fish to an isolation tank.

Shelter for fish

Fish need cover and shelter. When plants are dying back in the fall, replace the plant cover with alternatives, such as old drainpipes, old ceramic pots, bricks, or tiles—anything to put a roof over their heads.

Winter precautions

As fall turns to winter, remove the pump and fountain. Wash in warm, soapy water, then dry and wrap in newspaper. Store them in a dry, frostfree shed until the spring.

Semihardy plants can either be left to take their chances, or you can put them in containers and bring them indoors. Delicate floaters must be brought indoors.

Fountains

What are the options? Are pumps hard to source?

Not long ago, the options for fountains were limited, because water pumps were bulky, difficult to source, and very expensive. The pump machinery also needed to be set up in a shed. But it is now possible to get all manner of easy-to-fit, underwater electric pumps at a relatively low cost. Today, the scope of a fountain is limited only by the size of your bank balance, and designs ranging from the simplistic to the ambitious are within reach.

FOUNTAIN OPTIONS

There are two basic types of fountain: those where water is pushed up through an ornamental figure or form (statuette fountain), and those where the shape of the spray forms the decorative aspect (jet type). Within these two types, there are many options. Figures include nymphs, classical characters, and animals; forms encompass millstones, dishes, spouts, and many other unusual items. The spray patterns available with the jet type of fountain include everything from classic single sprays through to multi-tiered sprays, bell- and ring-shaped sprays, and bubbling and gushing geysers.

A traditional, high-quality fountain with a single surface spray—good for oxygenating a small pond without introducing an ornamental figure.

A broad, overflowing dish fountain with a single bubble geyser at its center—perfect for introducing the sights and sounds of moving water, while at the same time encouraging wildlife.

A large, pierced reconstituted stone fountain with a gushing geyser as a centerpiece—great for complementing a natural-looking pond.

JET PATTERNS

If you want to oxygenate a pond and at the same time enjoy the pleasures of moving water, yet without introducing an ornament, a simple jet-type fountain is the answer. There are dozens of different varieties on the market: some have the fountain head positioned above the water, others have it set underwater; some have moving parts to direct the spray.

| Single spray | Multi-spray | Gushing geyser | Ring spray | Bell spray | Double bell spray |

HOW TO SET UP A STATUETTE FOUNTAIN

↘ Using a large pot and some bricks, position the statuette so that the base is just below the surface of the water and the submersible pump is balanced on the bricks. Pass the power cable through a protective ribbed PVC pipe and site it so that it is hidden along its route and as it enters the pond.

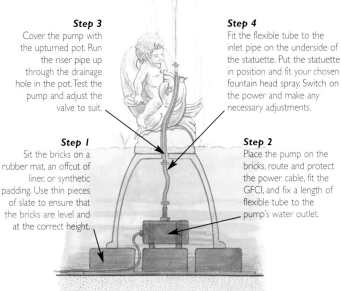

Step 3
Cover the pump with the upturned pot. Run the riser pipe up through the drainage hole in the pot. Test the pump and adjust the valve to suit.

Step 4
Fit the flexible tube to the inlet pipe on the underside of the statuette. Put the statuette in position and fit your chosen fountain head spray. Switch on the power and make any necessary adjustments.

Step 1
Sit the bricks on a rubber mat, an offcut of liner, or synthetic padding. Use thin pieces of slate to ensure that the bricks are level and at the correct height.

Step 2
Place the pump on the bricks, route and protect the power cable, fit the GFCI, and fix a length of flexible tube to the pump's water outlet.

A small ornamental fountain with a simple single-spray fountain head pulsing out of a delightful statuette. The sound of moving water is enjoyable and relaxing, and the oxygenated water helps to keep the pond in good condition. Even better, the whole project can be set up in a few hours.

Dos and don'ts

Fountains are beneficial and great fun, but only if well sited and working properly.

Do make sure that you choose the correct pump to suit your needs.

Do make sure that you fit an electrical circuit breaker, to prevent the risk of electric shock.

Do make sure that your pump and ornament are compatible, with adequate power and correct fittings.

Do make sure that the fountain is set level—check with a carpenter's level.

Don't stint on the amount of tubing to the extent that the tube is kinked and the flow of water impeded.

Don't have a complex, fine spray with a high profile on a windy site.

Don't choose a heavy spray if you have a display of broad-leaved surface plants such as water-lilies and lotuses.

PUMPS

There are two types of pump (submersible and surface-mounted). Submersible pumps are usually the best choice. High-voltage, surface-mounted pumps are certainly an option, but only if you need to shift huge quantities of water. The easiest way to work out the size of pump required is to measure the head height (distance from the surface of the water to the top of the fountain head), add 12 inches for good measure, then get a pump of that capacity. See also pages 18–19.

You will also need a good length of low-voltage, heavy-duty cable (enough to run from the pump cable to the house supply), a waterproof connector, an electrical circuit interrupter, and enough PVC conduit or ribbed pipe to protect the length of cable. If you are fitting the pump directly to the underside of an ornamental statuette, you will also need compatible fittings.

STAND-ALONE PATIO FOUNTAINS

If you want all the pleasures of moving water, but do not have or want a pond (perhaps you are worried about children's safety, want the set-up directly on a patio, or maybe you live in rented property where there are restrictions), then a pump-and-sump fountain kit is a good option. See also pages 75–77.

You need a sump (which will hold all the water), a submersible pump to fit the sump, an ornamental figure or form, an electrical circuit interrupter, and, of course, a fountain head. Make sure that you choose a fountain spray with a low profile, so that the water doesn't get blown all over the patio. If you do not want to upset the patio by digging a hole for the sump, you could instead opt for a decorative sump—a tank, pot, or barrel—that you can sit directly on the paving.

Traditional wall mask fountains or waterspouts are another possibility and a good choice for small patios (see pages 70–71).

Cascades and waterfalls

What is the difference between the two?

Awaterfall is a large body of water falling off a single shelf, while a cascade is a body of water falling down a series of shelves, rather like water running down a flight of stairs. In both features, water is pumped up to a header pool where it brims to overflowing. In a waterfall it spills over as a sheet, in a single dramatic drop from one level to another, while in a cascade, it brims over and splashes down from one step to another in a series of mini waterfalls.

CASCADE AND WATERFALL OPTIONS

Cascade or waterfall?

Do you want the water to fall the height of the drop—for example, 32 inches—in a single curtain, which will be noisy and dramatic? Or do you want the water to run down in steps—for example, four 8-inch steps?

What do you want at the bottom of the fall? Do you want the water to fall into a pond containing plants and fish (in which case a cascade is probably the best option), or is the drama of falling water enough in itself?

Remember that although a waterfall is exciting, the noise and movement of a single fall can become annoying. A cascade, on the other hand, is more restful.

Natural-looking or architectural?

Waterfalls and cascades can be constructed in one of two ways: either to imitate nature, with the whole layout built from real or reconstituted rocks and stones; or put together in a way that draws its inspiration from man-made forms, such as the overflow from a canal or reservoir.

Think about which approach most appeals to you and will also complement the style of your garden. You could have a miniature Niagara Falls complete with rock shelves, boulders, and shingle; or maybe you would prefer brickwork, perhaps with details in metal and stone.

Small cascades for the patio

It is possible to enjoy the spectacle of falling water on even the smallest patio.

Wall mask waterspout ~ A wall mask waterspout is a tidy solution if you want the effect of falling water, but have only a small patio. You can achieve a cascade effect by letting the water from the waterspout flow into one or more brimming bowls (see page 69).

Traditional cascade ~ There are many pump-and-sump designs that give the effect of water brimming over from one level to another, without the need to dig holes—pumps gushing into barrels, a pyramid of overflowing bowls, and many more besides (see page 75).

HOW TO BUILD A CASCADE

Cascade using preformed units

↘ Look at the units and measure them to find out the vertical drop and the horizontal run. Study the site and decide how many units you need to complete the project. Choose a pump and pipework to suit your situation.

Step 3
Use stone and mortar to bed the units in place. Run the pump to test the system.

Step 4
Run the outflow pipe into the top unit and hide it under a flat stone.

Step 2
Starting at the bottom, set the units in place so that they overlap one another.

Step 1
Position the pump in a pond or sump and run the outflow pipe to the header pool.

Cascade using flexible liner

↘ The cascade can be built either with a single large sheet of liner or with separate sheets for each tier. If you are building a cascade as a follow-up project to a pond, you may have leftover bits of liner that can be used.

Step 4
Use stone and mortar to cover the liner and make the steps look like natural outcrops.

Step 3
Cover the tiered steps with liner, so that it runs into the reservoir pool.

Step 2
Fit an optional filter unit (important if you want to have lots of exotic fish).

Step 1
Position the pump in a pond or sump and run the outflow pipe to the header pool.

HOW TO BUILD A WATERFALL

If you have an existing stream, you can easily build a permanent waterfall. Start by building a dam to divert the stream away from the site. To make the drop, dig a trench across the width of the stream and fill it with 6 inches of concrete. Lay a horizontal splash slab and build a vertical wall on this footing, as a base for the spillway. Select a large feature stone for the spillway and set it in place on a bed of mortar. Sit a flat rock on top of the spillway stone to create a generous overlapping lip. Disguise concrete with stone and shingle.

Step 2
Bed the spillway stone on mortar so that the top of the stone is level with the top of the wall.

Step 1
Dig a trench (deep enough to suit your site) and fill it with 6 inches of concrete. Build a concrete splash slab (6 inches thick) and a vertical wall (6 inches thick) behind this footing.

Step 3
Position a flat stone to form a lip that juts over the top of the spillway and concrete wall. Bed it in mortar.

Step 4
Cover the concrete with rocks and gravel.

Step 5
Continue landscaping the banks so that all traces of concrete are hidden.

Step 6
Finally, remove the dam and let the stream top up the header pool and run its course.

BUILDING A SLOPE

The easiest and most economical way of building a slope for a cascade or waterfall is to build the project as an addition to a pond, and use the spoil from the pond. This solves the problem of what to do with the spoil, and helps you to keep costs to the minimum.

PUMP POWER

Calculate the head height (vertical distance from the surface of the water in the reservoir to the top of the header pool), and then get the most powerful pump that you can afford.

REFINEMENTS

If you like the idea of cascades and ponds (and space and levels allow), it is possible to combine the two in the form of an extended stream made from a number of linked pools. All you do is build the ponds on linked terraces so that they lap into one another.

This can be refined further by filling up the ponds so that the system is working, and then excavating little flow-offs from the ponds to make bog areas for side planting.

Streams

Can I have a stream in my small garden?

It is possible to have a stream if your garden is big enough to contain a meandering necklace of small, thin, natural-looking ponds, and there is enough space to have a large header pool at the top end and a sizeable reservoir pool at the bottom end. You must be prepared for hard work, because there will be a lot of digging and moving of soil involved. To get the best effect, you also need room for a generous amount of planting alongside the stream.

A mountain stream is a stunning sight as it rushes vigorously downhill. The bare rocks suggest that the fast-flowing stream might at any moment become a torrent!

MOUNTAIN STREAM

Mountain streams are rocky, fast-flowing, and noisy. If you want a similar torrent, there are three requirements: you must have a dramatic sloping site, a powerful pump to cope with the volume and force of water required, and a good supply of rock for the base and banks of the stream.

MEADOW STREAM

A natural meadow stream or brook—the perfect choice for most gardens—is a slow-flowing, meandering strip of water with planting to the sides. The sights and sounds of water are therapeutic and lend themselves to meditation, but much of the attraction of a meadow stream is in the slow movement of the water, the shape of the curved banks, the heavy side planting of lush bog plants, and the richness of the associated wildlife.

CONSIDERING YOUR SITE

Natural streams tend to flow through valleys, with the land at each side of the stream forming a gently angled slope that runs down to the water. Look at your site and see if it is possible to excavate a generous, meandering ditch around trees and borders. Will you be able to spread the spoil over the garden to create a slope down to the water?

A slow-flowing meadow stream is a haven for wildlife and the perfect place for quiet reflection. A wide variety of plants add a palette of textures to its banks.

STREAM OPTIONS

Meadow stream

↘ A very slow-running stream winding through a meadow, with lush bog plants on its banks, grass running down to the water, and a layer of muddy sediment on its base.

Rocky mountain stream

↘ A fast-running stream gushing through a gulch, with lots of rocks to the sides, and areas of shale bordering the water. The base is made up of a mixture of sand, shingle, and layers of rock.

Dammed stream

↘ A stream made from a series of linked pools, with waterfalls running over dams. The project is planned so that each pool can survive as an independent unit if the pump fails.

HOW TO MAKE A STREAM

Step 5
Fill the stream with water (to overflowing) and set the pump working. Plant the sides of the stream with your chosen plants, bedding them in generous swathes that run in and out of the water.

Step 4
Rake and grade the spoil so that it covers the whole site, running down the banks and over the concrete to the center of the stream. Aim for gentle, smooth contours.

Step 3
Lay a 4-inch-thick layer of concrete over the synthetic padding and butyl rubber sandwich, making it a generous width that spreads beyond the edges of the sandwich.

Step 2
Build spillways or dams at each of the overflow lips between the trenches. Cover the whole excavation with a sandwich of synthetic padding, butyl rubber and synthetic padding.

Step 1
Mark out the route of the stream and excavate a series of wide, linked V-section trenches. Make the trenches about twice the width of the envisaged stream.

↙ Mark out the route and excavate a series of wide V-section linked plateaux or steps. Bury the water supply pipe so that it links the header and reservoir pools. Roll synthetic padding over the whole excavation, followed by butyl rubber liner and another layer of synthetic padding. Cover this "sandwich" with a 4-inch layer of concrete.

Make a firm spillway or dam at the point where the pools lap over each other. Position rocks on the pond side of each dam. Spread the spoil over the whole area so that there is a gentle slope down to the center of the stream.

Fit the pump and top up the whole system with water, so that you can see the water levels. Plant the sides of the stream with your favorite bog and meadow plants, such as irises, rushes, grasses, ferns, and marsh plants.

ADDITIONAL FEATURES FOR STREAMS

Stepping stones ~ These make a beautiful feature, drawing the eye to the width of the stream and the surrounding planting. It is best to bed the stones in mortar at the concreting stage of the stream's construction.

Bridges ~ A stream can be wonderfully embellished by a bridge. The act of crossing water and great swathes of plants by bridge gives the garden a new dimension.

Waterwheels ~ If you enjoy brickwork and stonework, a waterwheel is a fun idea. You would need to build a narrow gap into a spillway, with a bearing at each side to take the spindle; the waterwheel could be made from wood, with metal for the frame.

Stones for streams

Try to use local stone—the colors will be sympathetic to the environment and costs will be lower.

Use a single type of stone ~ For a natural effect, settle on one type of stone. Imitate nature by using a mixture of split stone for building up the banks, and weathered stones in the water.

Consider scale and arrangement ~ Try to reflect the character of your garden in your choice of stone. Use split stone and boulders for the overall scheme, with one or two "feature" stones for stepping stones and islands. A salvaged cut stone could be used to suggest a past history.

PLANTS FOR STREAMS

Look at a local natural stream for inspiration and use it as a guide.

Choose local varieties ~ Don't be tempted to plant a lot of wildly exotic species, as they may be hard to establish successfully.

Suitable plants ~ You need to be thinking about rushes, irises, grasses, and ferns, with perhaps small willows and one or two exotics thrown in for good measure. Start with plants that thrive in your area, so that you quickly establish a basic framework of color and texture, and then gradually introduce areas of feature planting. Ask the gardeners at local parks and gardens with streams for advice.

Bog gardens

What is a bog garden?

Natural wild ponds are characterized by soggy, low-lying areas around the water's edge, which are packed full of rushes, irises, the nests of wild fowl, frogs, newts, and so on. These areas never dry out and are so wet that they are always difficult underfoot, but the conditions are such that the water is free-flowing through the soil rather than stagnant. A bog garden is an artificial replication of this stretch of pond-side plant life.

A GREAT PLACE FOR PLANTING

Areas of moist ground are just perfect for planting a whole range of lush, water-loving plants. Houses are generally built on well-drained sites, so their gardens also tend to be well drained. The construction of a bog garden, therefore, will enable you to add a new kaleidoscope of exciting colors and textures to your gardening palette, with lots of rich greens, smooth, fleshy foliage, and dramatic leaf shapes.

WHERE CAN I PUT A BOG GARDEN?

Bog gardens can be built around the edge of a wildlife pond (so that they benefit from pond overflow and seepage), or they can be constructed in a separate area well away from the pond (indeed the garden does not need to have a pond at all). If you do not want to build a pond—because of the small size of your garden, or because you have children and are worried about their safety—you can settle for just making a bog garden.

Look for plants that enjoy damp conditions—plants that are associated with marshland, shady woodlands, low-lying riverbanks, and riverside meadows.

HOW TO MAKE A BOG GARDEN

A stand-alone bog garden
Built as an independent feature

↘ A bog garden can be created by lining a hole with plastic, adding shingle for drainage, and installing a water feed to ensure that the soil is kept damp. To cut costs, use black plastic bags lapped over each other to line the hole.

A bog garden by a pond
Built to extend a pond's visual impact

↘ A pond-side bog garden is best built at the same time as the pond, using offcuts of liner. The bog garden will benefit from constant seepage from the pond, but you do have to ensure that it doesn't leach nutrients back into the water.

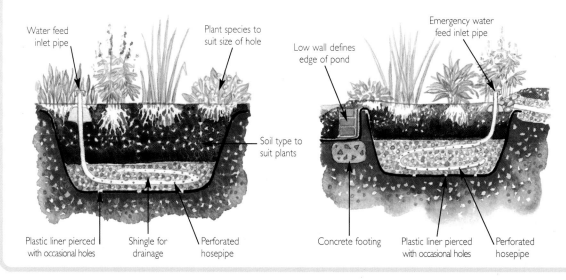

Water feed inlet pipe

Plant species to suit size of hole

Soil type to suit plants

Plastic liner pierced with occasional holes

Shingle for drainage

Perforated hosepipe

Emergency water feed inlet pipe

Low wall defines edge of pond

Concrete footing

Plastic liner pierced with occasional holes

Perforated hosepipe

BOG PLANTS

A luscious, unrestrained mixture of hardy pond-side and bog plants—arum lilies, montbretia, wild rushes, grasses, and irises—all of which enjoy the moist soil conditions.

Bog plants—sometimes described by nurseries as "moisture-loving plants"—positively enjoy being in damp, boggy soil, the proviso being that the water in the soil is free-moving. That is to say, while bog plants thrive in boggy soil, they are not so happy in soil that is waterlogged or has become stagnant.

Many shallow-water marginal plants can also be grown successfully in bog gardens.

Purchase a small number of plants to start with and read the labels carefully. Don't set the plants too deep, and be careful that the bog doesn't dry out or flood.

BOG PLANT TROUBLES

Bog plants require no more care than those in other parts of the garden. However, there are specific problems to watch out for.

Snail damage ~ Large numbers of water snails can munch through new plants. Get fish to limit the snail population.

Crown and leaf rot ~ If the crown of a new plant swiftly turns yellow, the likelihood is that it is unhappy with the depth of the water. Try lifting it to a slightly drier area.

Insect pests ~ Most insect pests can be controlled by rubbing them off with your fingers, or by spraying them off with a fine mist of water. Be wary of using insecticide because it may be lethal to fish. Always read the labels.

Popular bog plants

There are many plants that will grow in moist, boggy conditions, sometimes with their roots covered in water, but these conditions do have to be constant. It is no good if the soil condition swings between being boggy and being dry.

Generally good	Good flowers	Good foliage
Japanese iris *Iris kaempferi* Long, narrow leaves and blue, white, and purple flowers. Best grown in large clumps.	**Japanese primrose** *Primula japonica* "Miller's Crimson" Brilliant red-orange flowers. Good in wet, free-draining soil.	**Prickly rhubarb** *Gunnera manicata* Leaves up to 5 feet across. Needs space.
Giant rhubarb *Rheum palmatum rubrum* Giant leaves with red flowers. Needs lots of space.	**Globe flower** *Trollius* Golden flowers. Very attractive in swathes.	**Eulalia grass** *Miscanthus sinensis* "Zebrinus" Striking striped foliage.
Plantain lily *Hosta* Large, fleshy leaves with small drooping flowers. Looks very good when grouped. Easy to grow and adaptable.	**Tawny day lily** *Hemerocallis fulva* "Kwanso Flore Pleno" Rich orange flowers with rushlike leaves. Good in large clumps.	**Royal fern** *Osmunda regalis* Tall green fronds with spiky brown flowers.
Day lily *Hemerocallis* Rushlike foliage with a succession of little trumpet-like flowers. There are lots of types. Looks good in swathes by a pond.	**Lucifer montbretia** *Crocosmia* "Lucifer" Flame-red flowers and green leaves. Long-lasting flowers.	**Ribbon grass** *Phalaris arundinacea* "Picta" Green and white striped grass. **White false hellebore** *Veratrum album* Tall flowers. Good in large clumps.

MINIATURE BOG GARDENS

If you would like a bog garden but are short of space—perhaps you have only a balcony or a small roof garden—a container bog garden is the answer. You can create a really lush effect by looking for attractive containers and massing them in groups.

Soil to suit your plant. Plantpot with drainage holes

Water level adjusted to suit your chosen plant

Generous layer of clean, washed gravel or shingle

Glazed pot—the drainage holes are bunged with corks

Beaches and natural surrounds

I like pebbles— would a beach be hard to build?

In the context of a pond, a beach is defined as a wide strip of rounded pebbles or shingle that runs in a gentle slope from the land to the water. The beauty of a beach is that you can walk down to the water's edge without getting your feet muddy and without fear of slipping in. A beach isn't any more difficult to build than a grassy slope, for instance (in many ways it is easier), although the site needs to be larger, more forward planning is required, and it is more expensive.

BEACHES

Building a beach around a pond in a large garden is a great idea. The slow slope down to the water is safe and firm underfoot. Children and older people cannot easily slip into the water, there is no mud for dogs, chickens, and children to churn up, and it makes a good base for using wheelbarrows, toys, and garden furniture.

The only downside of a beach that encircles a pond is that a gentle slope does require a lot of space. You cannot lessen the amount of space needed by having a sudden steep slope—the gravel would slide into the water and it would become slippery and dangerous.

One space-saving solution is to design the pond so that there is a gently sloping beach on one side and a bog garden or area of planting on the other. This arrangement means that you get the best of both worlds—you can walk right down to the water's edge to view the water, and also enjoy the plants on the other side of the pond.

OTHER NATURAL SURROUNDS

If you don't favor a shingle beach, there are other possibilities. You could use slate, stone, sand, or bark. Maybe a wide band of bog garden with rushes, a meadow coming right down to the water's edge, or even a surround made up of found feature items such as moss-covered tree roots or boulders might be more to your liking.

Spend time exploring the suppliers in your area to see what's on offer. This will help you to keep costs down to a minimum and better still, the use of local materials will ensure that the character of the pond will be in harmony with its environs.

An area of smooth, multicolored pebbles beside a pond enables you to get close to the water without worrying about getting your feet wet or muddy, and looks attractive.

Additional props

Look at the surroundings of any natural stretch of water and you will see clues about the way it is used. You too can add items—either to paint a scene or for fun.

Things you can create ~ You could build a pier to jut out from a beach, or perhaps have a row of groynes running down to the water. You could grade the shingle from large pebbles to sand.

Things you can look out for ~ You could theme your pond—a pond with a beach could have an old rowboat or a pile of netting and lobster pots; a farmyard-type pond could be decorated with wagon wheels, old tools, cattle troughs, fencing, or tree stumps.

A modest garden pond bordered by bog plants on one side, backed by an interesting selection of shrubs. Compacted gravel gives a clean profile to the rest of the pond.

HOW TO MAKE A POND AND BEACH

↘ Dig a large hole, edge it with bricks, and line it with synthetic padding and butyl rubber, just as for a natural pond. The only difference is that instead of a flat planting shelf which runs from the edge of the pond to the start of the 3-in-1 slope to the bottom of the pond (see page 13), there is a long, slow slope from the garden to the edge of the pond, continuing across a much wider strip than the planting shelf would have occupied. The aim is to hide the pond edge under the beach.

When ordering the gravel for the beach, make sure that you specify well-washed, rounded gravel. It must not be dirty or salty. Do not use crushed stone. If you want an extra-special beach, order three sizes of gravel, ranging from egg-size stones down to pea-size pebbles, and lay it so the sizes are graded, with the smallest size by the water.

Tapered concrete retaining wall (8 inches thick)

Step 4
Clip away the synthetic padding and wrap the edge of the butyl rubber over the top of the wall.

Step 5
Place a ring of large stones around the base of the 3-in-1 slope, to prevent the gravel from sliding down into the depths.

Step 6
Grade the gravel so that it runs in a gradual slope from the garden over the wall and shelf, and comes to a halt against the ring of stones.

Concrete footing (8 inches thick)

Step 3
Cover the site with synthetic padding and butyl rubber, and build a wall (three bricks high) around what will be the edge of the water.

Step 2
Grade a wide, long, gradual slope that runs from the garden down to the 3-in-1 slope that descends to the depths of the pond.

Step 1
Clear the topsoil and dig the hole to the depth of the pond.

HOW TO MAKE A "RIVER" WITH ROCKY BANKS

Step 3
Build a three-brick-high wall on the ring footing, to define the edge of the pond. Spread the synthetic padding and butyl rubber over the site, with an extra top layer of synthetic padding over the area in front of the wall.

Step 4
Spread mortar on the synthetic padding and bed the rocks in place so that the synthetic padding and butyl rubber run up between the rocks and the wall.

↓ This project is only a river in the sense that its ends are hidden from view, and its length is much greater than its width. The rocks need to be positioned so that they are partially submerged in the water. The river is built in much the same way as the natural pond, with synthetic padding and butyl rubber, the only difference being that the narrow planting shelf is replaced by a concrete slab topped with a retaining wall and large rocks.

Step 2
Dig a trench and lay a concrete ring footing (8 inches thick), making it wide enough to support both the retaining wall and rocks.

Step 1
Mark out the river and dig out the area, complete with a shelf and a 3-in-1 slope that runs down to the depths.

Step 5
Trim the synthetic padding and butyl rubber so that they are below ground level. Spread the soil so that it meets the back of the rocks.

Bridges and stepping stones

I'd love a bridge—are they hard to build?

A bridge over water can transform a garden: it is an irresistible invitation both to cross the water from one part of the garden to another, and to pause on the bridge to enjoy the view. Such crossings vary in complexity, from basic stepping stones to straightforward sleeper bridges and more involved bridge structures.

Ways to cross water

The width and depth of the water decides the design of the water crossing.

- A single railroad tie makes the perfect crossing for a narrow rivulet.
- A wider stream requires two beams with planks fixed across them.
- Deep and wide streams need a bridge with handrails, both for safety and structural integrity.
- Flat stepping stones suit a slow-flowing, shallow rivulet or stream.
- As an alternative to a bridge for crossing a wide stretch of deep water, stone slabs set on piers can be used. Drain the water to make the building process easier.

STEPPING STONES

Natural stones

↗ *A single row of found, natural stepping stones—a good choice for a simple, shallow stream. The flat stones can be positioned to suit the location.*

Japanese stones

↗ *This looks like a large body of water punctuated by an arrangement of stones, but in fact there is very little water.*

Stones for deep water

↗ *Paving slabs bedded on top of brick-built piers—for crossing wide, deep water.*

HOW TO MAKE A SLEEPER BRIDGE

A small sleeper bridge spanning boggy ground—practical, attractive, and straightforward to make.

Step 2
Depending upon the site and levels, use blocks or bricks to build little piers on the footing slabs at each side of the stream, making them level with each other.

Step 3
Set the ties to span the two piers, easing them into position and bedding them on a generous spread of mortar.

Step 4
Build a path up to the ends of the ties, with one or more steps as necessary.

Step 1
Dig a shallow trench (12 inches deep) and fill it with 8 inches of concrete. Do this on both sides of the stream.

Step 6
If you are unsure on your feet, fix a simple handrail alongside one of the ties.

Step 5
If you are worried about slipping, cover the ties with wire netting.

HOW TO BUILD AN ARCHED BRIDGE

One of the simplest designs to build is a wooden arched bridge, with eight support posts, a cross-plank footway, and handrails to both sides. The main beams are linked to the posts via cross-beams, and bound together with cross-planks; the handrails are built up from the ends of the posts. The U-shaped form (seen in end section) is strong, stable, and attractive. The rails not only make for a safer crossing, but also help to make the structure rigid.

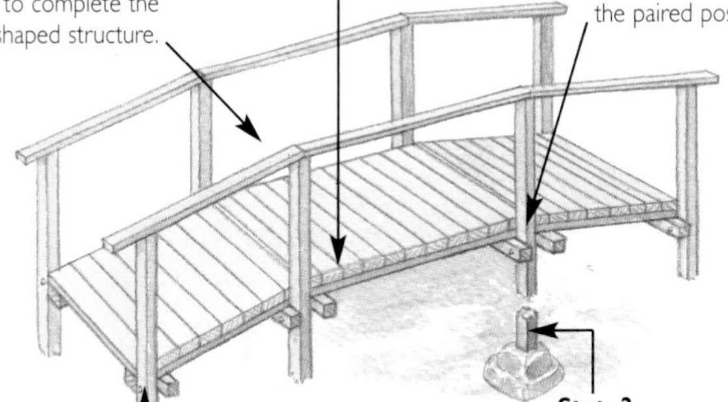

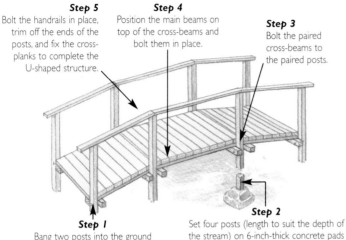

Step 5
Bolt the handrails in place, trim off the ends of the posts, and fix the cross-planks to complete the U-shaped structure.
Step 4
Position the main beams on top of the cross-beams and bolt them in place.
Step 3
Bolt the paired cross-beams to the paired posts.
Step 1
Bang two posts into the ground at either side of the stream.
Step 2
Set four posts (length to suit the depth of the stream) on 6-inch-thick concrete pads laid directly on the bed of the stream.

MORE WOODEN BRIDGES

A traditional U-form (seen in end section) bridge with cross-ties and handrails. Three ties have been extended to make outriggers to support the posts and rails.

A simple bridge in the Japanese folk tradition. The little beams that link the bottom ends of the posts to the main beams help keep the handrail strong and stable.

ARCHED BRIDGES IN BRICK AND STONE

Traditional brick and stone arched bridges are efficient, long-lasting structures, which are delightful to look at. However, they are very complex structures to build, because wooden formers are needed to take the weight of the stone while the bridge is being built. But if you have a small, deep stream, you can build such a bridge by rolling a large concrete pipe into the water, and using this as a permanent former that is left in place. You simply build a path to run up and over the pipe, so that the pipe is hidden.

A simple arched bridge built in stone over a large concrete pipe. The pipe is rolled into the stream and left in place.

HOW TO BUILD A STONE PACK BRIDGE

The stone pack or post bridge dates back to early times when packhorses were used to transport goods. In effect, such bridges are a series of stone piers linked by large slabs of stone, with the height and spacing of the piers governed by the depth of the water and the length of the spanning slabs. If you want to build a similar bridge for your garden, decide first how big a slab you can lift, and find out whether such slabs are readily available in your area.

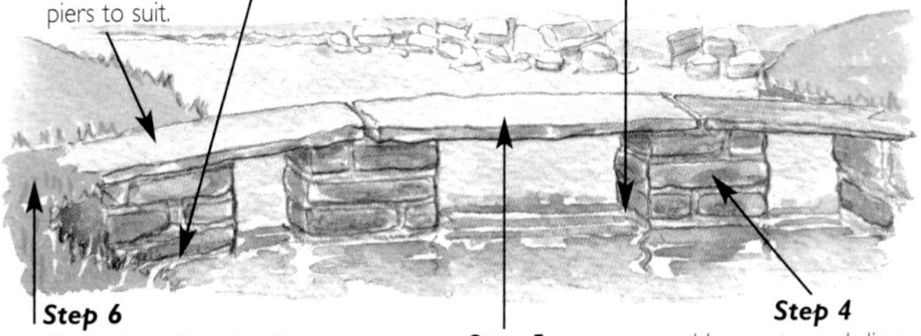

Step 1
Drain the stream. Measure the length of your stone slabs and mark out the position of the piers to suit.
Step 2
In 12-inch-deep holes at either side of the water, lay 6-inch-thick concrete footing slabs directly on the ground.
Step 3
Build 6-inch-thick concrete footing slabs directly on the bed of the stream, at several places across the water, to match the length of your slabs.
Step 6
Grade the soil so that it runs smoothly up to the slab on both sides of the water, making a firm path up to the start of the bridge.
Step 5
When the mortar has set and the piers are stable, set the spanning slabs on generous beds of mortar.
Step 4
Use mortar and slices of stone to build the piers up to the same height. Make sure that they are upright and level.

Piers and decking

How do piers and decking differ?

The best definition of a pier or jetty is a narrow wooden walkway that extends over a stretch of water such as sea, a large lake or a pond. Decking is more of a wooden patio that may or may not be built beside water. Both are made of wood and elevated, and the wonderful thing about them is that the movement of soil during the building process can be kept to a minimum—they fly over difficult terrains such as rocky slopes, bogs, and, of course, water.

Very stable, L-shaped pond-side decking, with the long arm of the "L" running out across the water to form a pier.

WOODEN PLATFORMS

Waterside platforms must be constructed so that they do not affect the integrity of the pond—with no poisons leaching off treated wood, or posts doing damage to pond liners. The bearers need to be about 16–20 inches apart so that they don't sag. The posts must be cut back to take the bearers, so that the weight of the bearers is borne on a step. Finally, the bearers need to be bolted to the posts, and the planks screwed or nailed to the bearers.

Decking set alongside a pond is a great place from which to enjoy the water. This decking cleverly conceals a water pump and filter system for the pond.

HOW TO MAKE A PIER

This pier is built in much the same way as an area of decking—the legs are set into underwater concrete footing slabs or pads (which are supported on thick mats made up of synthetic padding and butyl rubber). The mats help to spread the load and prevent the legs from doing damage to the liner. It is easiest if you can drain the pond, but otherwise you have to cast concrete pads onto the legs, and then have someone in the water to guide the resultant "feet" into place on the protective mats. It is difficult, but good fun.

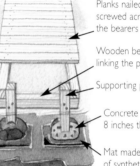

Planks nailed or screwed across the bearers

Wooden bearer linking the posts

Supporting posts

Concrete pad, 8 inches thick

Mat made up of synthetic padding and butyl rubber

HOW TO MAKE DECKING

Pond-side decking is built very close to the water, with the leading edge projecting at least 24 inches, so that the edge of the water is hidden by the decking platform. If you want to build decking alongside an existing pond, and you don't want to mess around with the integrity of the pond, the best way forward is to construct a low wall at the water's edge, and then build the decking so that the main bearers are anchored to the land and extend over the wall, rather like a diving board.

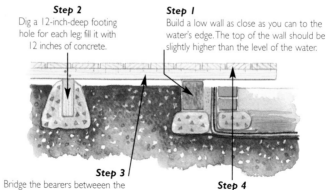

Step 2
Dig a 12-inch-deep footing hole for each leg; fill it with 12 inches of concrete.

Step 1
Build a low wall as close as you can to the water's edge. The top of the wall should be slightly higher than the level of the water.

Step 3
Bridge the bearers between the legs and the wall, so that they hang over the water.

Step 4
Fix the planks across the bearers—two screws or nails at each plank–bearer intersection.

Islands

An island can consist of anything from a mound that is almost as large as the pond itself (so that you have a hillock with a stream running round it, rather like a castle moat), through to a scrap of land that only has standing room for a couple of ducks. Whatever its size, the joy of an island is its inaccessibility. It could be created with the intention of making a miniature wildlife haven, or a refuge for frogs and newts. It could even become the focus for quiet reflection.

I have a small pond—can I have an island?

ISLAND OPTIONS

If you are building a pond and want an island as a primary feature, leave a mound and build the pond around it. If the island is to be a secondary feature, complete the pond and then build an island at its center.

Natural-looking bump

➘ If you want to build a natural pond complete with an island, and your garden is big enough to take a large pond, start by digging out the pond shape, leaving an island mound behind. Treat the edge of the island in the same way as the edge of the pond, by building a retaining wall (see pages 14–15, 26–27).

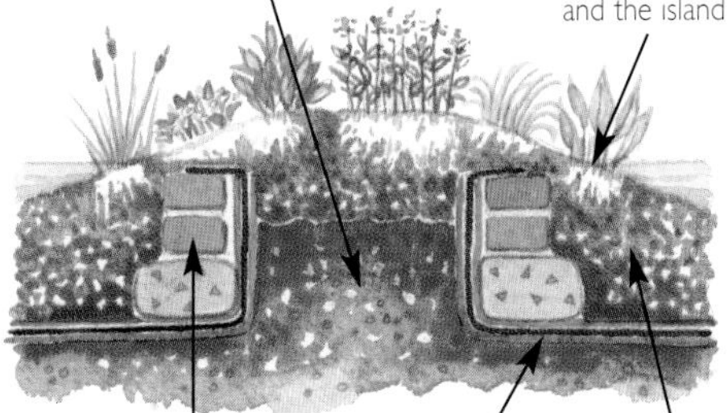
Pond dug out leaving a mound at its center
Planting shelves built around the pond and the island
Brick retaining walls around the pond and the island
Synthetic padding and butyl rubber liner spread over the whole site
Soil spread over the liner and retaining walls

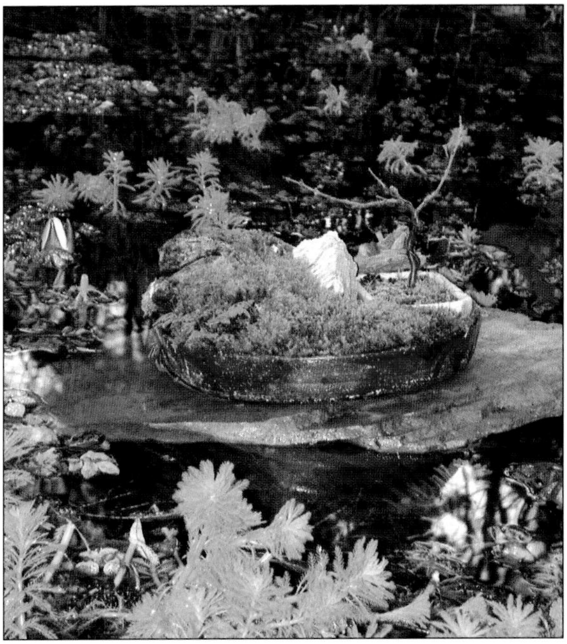

A mini pond gains extra character with the addition of a small, natural-looking stone island that displays a bonsai.

Building a plinth

For an existing pond, drain the water, establish the size and position of the plinth, spread a mat of synthetic padding and butyl rubber over the site, and cast a 6-inch-thick concrete pad on top, slightly larger than the plinth. Build a ring wall (size and depth to suit your pond) on the pad. Fill the center with rubble topped with soil.

For a new pond, dig out the pond, cast a concrete footing slab (6 inches thick and slightly larger than the plinth), spread the synthetic padding and butyl rubber over the site, and continue with the wall as described.

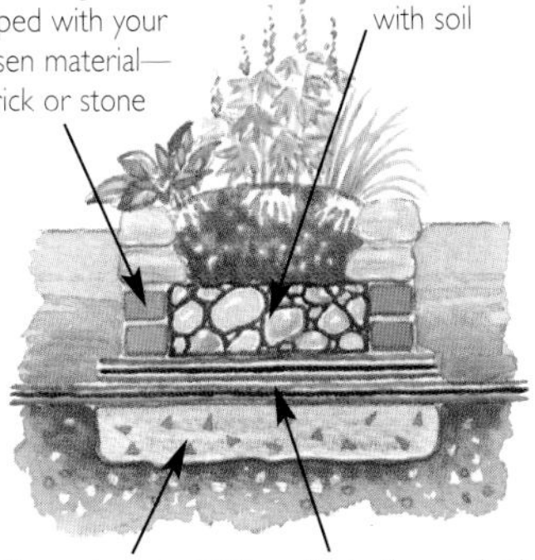
Brick ring wall topped with your chosen material—brick or stone
Rubble topped with soil
Concrete pad, slightly larger than the plinth and 6 inches thick
Protective synthetic padding either side of the butyl rubber liner

More island ideas

Sandbags in an existing pond ~ Drain the pond. Fill polypropylene bags with sand and build a ring wall with sides that angle in, rather like a truncated pyramid (for extra strength). Top the enclosure with soil.

Containers in an existing pond ~ Stand ceramic containers of plants on bricks or blocks. Adjust the levels to suit the needs of the plants.

Floating duck-house island ~ Build an open-sided, raft-size box and fill it with plastic containers. Float the raft in the pond and anchor it in position with at least two mooring weights. Build a kennel-like house for the ducks.

Sculpture for ponds

What makes a good sculpture?

Asculpture can be anything that captures your imagination—from the traditional, such as a classical nude figure, to more off-the-wall choices such as a brightly painted concrete block, an old iron wheel, or a pile of old watering cans. If you like it, and it won't annoy the neighbors or pollute the pond, then it is suitable. Look for items in garden centers, builder's yards, sawmills, art galleries, scrap metal yards, and architectural salvage yards.

SOME POPULAR POND ORNAMENTS

Special rock	Japanese crane	Classical figure	Japanese lantern

A rock fountain, used to suggest a natural spring—a place for quiet meditation.	*In Japan, cranes symbolize long life and are associated with quiet pleasure.*	*This figure of Pan is perfectly at home in a watery environment.*	*In a Japanese garden, a lantern represents a guide that lights our way.*

POND SCULPTURE OPTIONS

Figurative
A lifelike figure

↘ There is always something uniquely inspirational about a lifelike sculpture, whether it is a classical figure, a child, an animal, or a bird. Seek out a detailed sculpture that makes you feel good when you look at it.

Abstract
A symbolic sculpture

↘ A good abstract sculpture should set you wondering about what it represents. In the water sculpture illustrated, why are the fins set like a wheel with two fins higher than the rest? Is it meant to be a snail's shell?

Boulders, standing stones, fossils, driftwood, and tree trunks
Found items that are a celebration of nature

↘ The easiest sculptures to understand are those gathered from nature. Who can question a piece of driftwood, a moss-covered stone, or an ancient fossil? It is not pretending to be anything other than itself. If you found the item—perhaps on your last vacation, or in the course of your work—and it reminds you of a special time or place, it has extra value.

Making your own pond sculptures

Model your own ~ If you have always wanted to have a go at sculpture, this is the perfect opportunity. You could make a sculpture in clay and have it fired or cast. You could model your own figurative or abstract form in cement, fiberglass, or plaster.

Assemble found objects ~ You can make a sculpture from an assembly of components such as small stones or pieces of machinery. Consider looking for a stone column, a couple of slabs, and a few interesting little stones, and then build a Japanese lantern.

SCULPTURE WITHOUT A POND

If you like the idea of using sculpture but don't want a pond because it is too expensive or dangerous for children, build a pump-and-sump sculpture (see Small Water Features, pages 66–79).

Birds

One of the joys of a pond is that it attracts a wide range of wildlife. Just about everything that wiggles, crawls, swims, and flies is attracted by water. Algae flourishes in the warm water, small insects thrive on the algae, dragonflies eat the insects, and so it continues. The end result of this "eat-and-be-eaten" chain is that you get to see all manner of wonderful creatures, especially birds. If you supply the pond, nature will supply the birds.

I love birds—how do I attract them to my pond?

IDEAS FOR ATTRACTING BIRDS TO YOUR POND

Perching stones ~ Set rocks around the pond so that birds such as thrushes can use them to break open snails.

Shallow water ~ A gently sloping area of shallow water is good for ducks and for small birds to bathe.

Shelter ~ A low shelter (like a small dog kennel or upturned half-barrel) makes most birds feel secure.

Bird table ~ Make a habit of putting out scraps on a bird table.

A natural pond complete with a wooden raft and a duck decoy—fun to look at, and perfect for attracting wild ducks.

BIRD-FRIENDLY PONDS

Birds like a natural pond with lots of mud and plenty of warm, shallow water. Plant the surrounds of the pond with a wide variety of rushes, ferns, and grasses. If you are really keen, you can buy pond snails from a water garden center. Dense planting will attract lots of frogs, newts, and insects, water snails will eat all the plant debris and help keep the water clear, and birds will come along and do their best to eat the lot. Never let fertilizers leach into the pond, and keep weedkillers and chemical sprays well away.

KEEPING DUCKS

There are realities to face up to if you are considering getting ducks. Ducks are great fun. Their behavior is amusing, ducklings are wonderful to watch, and they are safe to have near children. But against that, you need to get a pair of ducks, and two ducks need plenty of space. They make a lot of mess both in and out of the water, their big, flat feet damage pond-side plants, and you need to be around to lock them in a duck house at night and let them out in the morning.

When you are searching out wood to make a duck house, or looking to buy a ready-made duck house, make sure that the wood is either untreated or treated with a preservative that is completely harmless to fish, plants, water, and, of course, ducks. Don't get the housing until you have decided on the breed of duck to buy—such as Pekin, Aylesbury, or Muscovy—and then choose a design that suits the size and character of the breed.

Top-quality houses for ducks and water fowl, made by a specialist company. Note the way the houses are mounted in or near the water so that they deter would-be predators. Some of the houses are fitted with automatic dusk–dawn door mechanisms.

Transforming existing ponds

My pond is terrible—can I give it a facelift?

It is always possible to breathe life into an existing pond. Whatever the condition of your pond—it might be made of low-grade **PVC** or concrete that has cracked, emptying the pond, or it might be full of mud and weed—it can be born again. It could well be hard, messy work, and you might find yourself up to your knees in mud, or crawling around saving gasping fish, but then again, that's half the fun and excitement of having a pond in the garden, isn't it?

IDEAS FOR TRANSFORMING A POND

Don't be disheartened if your pond looks tired, with broken edging or tatty concrete paving, because it can be rescued.

- If you have a natural pond with broken pavers around the edge, replace them with bands of planting.

- If it is a natural pond, identify which side brims over when it rains, and build a bog garden on that side to benefit from the wet conditions—you will end up with lots of lush plants.

- Build decking or a patio on the sunny side of the pond.

- Cover the pond surrounds with cobblestones and shingle for a beach.

- Install a water feature, such as a fountain or a Japanese deer scarer. Or build an additional pond to the side, with a waterfall to link the two ponds.

- If you are a parent or grandparent, you could empty the pond and fill it with sand to make a sandpit.

CLEANING

If your concrete or butyl rubber-lined pond is watertight but crammed with plants and full of debris, it needs to be cleaned out. Start by removing the container plants. Pick off all the algae and gently wash the plants under running water. Use a plastic bucket to scoop the mud out of the pond. Put the fish, snails, and frogs into an old tank or bath for safekeeping. Wash out the pond. Finally, refill the pond and carefully replace the plants and wildlife.

CHANGING THE POND EDGE AND SURROUNDING AREA

Edges and surfaces

➔ One of the swiftest ways of changing a pond is by remodeling the edge and the immediate surround. A thin, mean edging of broken concrete pavers could become a beach with decking attached; a messy grass strip could become a patio, and so on.

POND SURROUND OPTIONS

Natural ~ A natural surround might take the form of a bog with lush planting, a beach with cobblestones and shingle, or rocks with areas of ferns, grass, and mosses.

Brick and pavers ~ These will achieve a functional, architectural design, which will blend with features such as patios and walls.

Wood ~ Wood might be used in the form of fallen trees (as with a Japanese pond), or in the form of railroad ties and lumber, to create decking and piers inspired by the structures of the past.

↗ *A broken edging of pavers transformed by a beach and a pond-side decking with groups of feature rocks and container plants.*

Plants beside the pond

Badly designed, formal sunken ponds, with pavers around the edge, are a common problem. The easiest way to reinvigorate them is to strip away the pavers, and then to sculpt soil over the edge of the pond and introduce areas of heavy planting. Use the planting to blur the edges of the pond, so that it blends in with its surroundings. Let one side of the pond overflow, and this area can become a bog garden.

↗ *A badly designed, formal sunken pond is brought to life with a lush bog garden and lawn that comes down to the water.*

Ornaments and sculpture

Change a dull pond surround into something exciting and dynamic by making judicious additions.

See page 66 for container features. See pages 70–71 for waterspouts. See pages 76–77 for sculptural water features, and pages 78–79 for DIY creative sculptures.

RENOVATING THE STRUCTURE OF AN OLD NATURAL POND

If the pond is leaking (whether it is made of concrete or from a low-grade PVC), the best and longest lasting option is to reline it with butyl rubber. The procedure is to clean out the entire pond and scrub it clean. Remove anything sharp-edged or pointed. Remove the edging. Cover the whole area with a layer of synthetic padding followed by the butyl rubber. Cover the edges of the butyl rubber with offcuts of synthetic padding. Bury the edges of the liner, then remodel the soil and replant the surrounds so that the edge of the liner is concealed. Refill and restock the pond.

REDUCING, ENLARGING, AND RESHAPING PONDS

You can reduce the size of a pond by filling in part of it with rocks, planting, or a sculpture, or you can cover part of it with decking.

There are lots of ways to enlarge a pond—you can empty it out and start again, build pond-side bog gardens to give the effect of a much larger pond, construct another pond hard up against the first, or add various water features such as waterfalls and fountains.

To reshape a pond, follow any of the options just described. The most exciting way of enlarging and reshaping a pond is to build a second pond butting against the first, but at a slightly lower level. The water will brim over to create a weir.

REPLANTING OR REMOVING PLANTS

Sometimes a pond ends up with an imbalance of plants, such as too many irises, or too much parrotfeather. Of course, if you like irises and they obviously do well, you could concentrate on that species and search out every known type and color to build up a special collection. Otherwise, wait until the fall and then remove some of the dominant plants and bring in other varieties.

HANDLING AND REMOVING FISH

If the fish look happy—rolling and breeding in warm weather and generally increasing in number—leave them alone. If you do need to remove fish from a pond, gently scoop them up in a net and ease them out into a bucket of pond water. Cover the bucket with a damp towel. Return them to the pond as soon as possible.

WHEN IS A POND BETTER LEFT ALONE?

If fish are flourishing, plants are multiplying, and wildlife seems fine, leave the pond alone. Even if a pond has perhaps too many rushes, and the frogs have got out of hand, it may be better to accept it as it is. There is something really enchanting about an old pond that looks as if it hasn't been touched for 50 years.

ADAPTING PONDS TO PROTECT CHILDREN

Nothing is as important as the safety of children. Here are some ideas for making existing ponds safer, or for converting them.

- Put a child-proof fence around the whole pond, complete with a lock.

- Introduce ducks and a duck house to the pond-side, and surround the whole area with a fence and locked gate to keep children out.

- Cover the pond with a close mesh grid anchored just below the water level. Make sure that it is strong enough to support a child's weight.

- Extend the boundaries of the pond so that there is a big area of mud to cross before a child can get to the water.

- Fill the pond with soil and turn it into a large bog garden.

- Fill the pond with sand and turn it into a children's sandpit.

Remember: there are few second chances when it comes to children and water. A child can drown in moments. ALWAYS BUILD IN SAFEGUARDS!

POND FEATURES

A pond can be transformed by an additional feature. Fountains look good and will oxygenate the water, helping keep the water clear and enabling plants to flourish. Pond ornaments, such as a figure or a bird bath, can dramatically alter a pond's visual impact. Cascades or waterfalls will oxygenate the water and add new sights and sounds—a good option for uninspiring ponds.

Fountain

A sculpture with a spray fountain looks exciting and oxygenates the water (see pages 48–49).

Pond ornaments

Pond-side ornaments, such as a bird bath and container plants, add interest (see also pages 76–79).

Cascades and waterfalls

A cascade or waterfall will transform a tired pond—perfect if you like moving water (see pages 50–51).

Container ponds

My garden is minute, but can I still have a pond?

If you are really keen to build a water feature, yet your garden is very small—perhaps it is a city yard, minute balcony, or tiny patio where there is hardly room to sit, let alone build a pond—a container pond is the answer. If there is space for a half-barrel, cistern, old sink, trough, or even a group of large ceramic pots, there is sufficient room for a fully functioning miniature container pond complete with plants, which will soon attract wildlife.

Grouped potted plants, both inside and alongside a container pond, combine for interesting effect and are a good option if you have only a patio or terrace garden.

PREPARING CONTAINERS

Wooden barrels

↘ Look for a genuine oak half-barrel with iron hoops. Drive in screws just below the hoops, to hold them in place. Soak the barrel in water until the wood swells within the hoops, making the barrel watertight.

Ceramic pots

Look for a wide-rimmed pot, glazed inside and out, without a hole in the bottom (if it has, bung it up with a cork and fill with water until the cork swells and the pot is watertight). Repeatedly fill with water over a seven-day period, to remove debris and glazing chemicals, before stocking.

Oak staves angled so that they fit side by side

Iron hoops screwed in place to stop them sliding down

Use a genuine half-barrel with hoops and shaped staves, not one of the badly made imitations.

PLANTING A CONTAINER POND

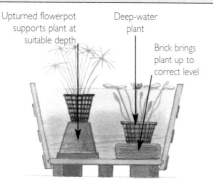

Upturned flowerpot supports plant at suitable depth

Deep-water plant

Brick brings plant up to correct level

↗ Set the container on three bricks, so that it is standing clear of the ground, and fill it with water until it is three-quarters full. Put one or more upturned flowerpots or bricks in the water to create planting shelves at the recommended level for your chosen water plants. Put the potted plants on the shelves.

CONTAINER POND PLANTS

Hornwort (*Ceratopyllum demersum*) ~ Deciduous perennial oxygenator, whorls of forked leaves.

Japanese cow-lily (*Nuphar japonica*) ~ Deciduous perennial floating plant with bright yellow flowers.

Blue flag (*Iris versicolor*) ~ Deciduous perennial marginal with violet-blue flowers.

Most floating plants (see page 41) are also suitable.

MORE CONTAINER POND IDEAS

Cauldrons, buckets, bathtubs, and other discarded household items make ideal ponds.

If you enjoy using salvaged items, look for old metal buckets, bathtubs; sinks, watering cans, WC pans, milk churns, and plastic garbage cans. If an item holds water, it is suitable for a container pond. If the container is very deep, like a milk churn, for example, a deep-water plant will be happy in it. Clusters of containers look very effective—such as several old pans, grouped with additional potted plants.

Wells, fonts, and troughs

In times gone by, many people worked on the land and lived in small, tight-knit rural communities. The landscape consisted of cottages, orchards, meadows, and hayricks. Wells, fonts, and troughs are reminiscent of this era. A good part of traditional garden design is concerned with creating evocative, three-dimensional scenes, and a garden well complete with a shingle roof, a winding handle, and a plunge bucket speaks a thousand words.

Why are wells, fonts, and troughs so special?

HOW TO BUILD A DECORATIVE WELL

A good well needs to be about 24–36 inches in diameter and built from brick. Dig a plastic garbage can into the ground so that the rim is at ground level. Dig a 12 x 12 inch trench around the can's rim and fill it with concrete. Build a waist-high brick wall off this footing. Fill the garbage can with water and add oxygenating plants to complete the illusion of a deep, dank well.

Step 3
Build a circular brick wall off this footing, with all the bricks set on edge, so that the face of the wall is made of header ends.

Step 2
Dig a trench around the outside of the garbage can rim, making it 12 inches deep and 12 inches wide. Fill the trench with concrete.

Step 1
Dig a hole deep enough to take a heavy-duty plastic garbage can, so that the rim ends up at ground level.

Step 4
Use reclaimed wood to build a gable roof. Pivot the winding beam between the two posts.

Step 5
Cover the roof with reclaimed shingles or old red roofing tiles.

CAUTION
Most children are fascinated by wells, especially if they are deep, dark, and a little scary. If you have children, fit a heavy wooden cover with a hasp and lock.

MORE ABOUT WELLS

There are as many designs for wells as there are old cottage gardens. Some are flush with the ground and fitted with a hand pump and trough, while others have a roof and are surrounded by a little picket fence.

If you want to perfect the illusion of an old, traditional well in your garden, you can dress the scene with an old wooden bucket, lots of heavy-duty rope, and a big wooden windlass with a winding handle.

Reclaiming attractive water containers

If you are looking for old water containers, visit a reclamation yard or, better still, a farm sale—old sinks, cisterns, and water troughs are just perfect. Don't worry if a lead cistern has a hole in it, because it can be mended easily. If you live in a city, you can perhaps search out an industrial tank from the time before plastics became common (the 1940s or earlier). If a container has held anything that may be damaging, have it checked out.

IDEAS FOR USING FONTS AND TROUGHS

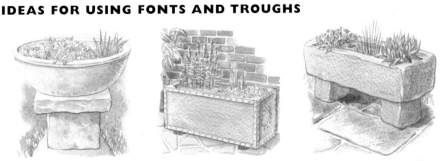

A sink with a hypertufa (moss, sand, and cement) covering looks like an old stone trough.

A salvaged stone bowl is set waist-high on a stone column to look like a church font.

An old, galvanized water cistern set on brick plinths in order to look more impressive.

A genuine carved stone coffin trough creates a charming scene in any landscape.

Pebble fountains

A pebble fountain is best defined as a small, self-contained, pump-and-sump fountain that uses cobblestones, pebbles, and gravel as its main feature. Pebble fountains are a uniquely beautiful combination of stone and running water, inspired by nature—think of water washing over shingle on a sun-drenched beach, dragging the stones in a swishing rumble, pebbles glinting on a shallow river bed, or crystal-clear water running over smooth stones in a mountain stream.

IDEAS AND OPTIONS

Pebble fountains are sight and sound pictures that use natural wonders such as the sea, springs, and streams as a reference. The whole idea of a pebble fountain is to build a stone and water sculpture that makes you feel at peace. There are thousands of possibilities—water running down the face of a large rock, water splashing and bubbling over a heap of pebbles, or water playing over a piece of worked stone such as a hewn basin or an old millstone. Think back to your childhood and remember the simple pleasures of water play; recreate this enjoyment by installing a pump-and-sump fountain and observing the interplay between the pebbles and the water—great effects from a simple set-up.

Pebble fountains are a particularly good option if you have young children, as they are much safer structures than a pond. This fountain has a log surround, which blends perfectly into a "woodland" area of the garden.

HOW TO BUILD A PEBBLE FOUNTAIN

↙ ↘ A pebble fountain consisting of stones in a range of sizes (left). To make your own boulder from hypertufa (a mixture of sand, cement, and sphagnum moss), simply dig a boulder-shaped hole in the ground, push a copper tube into it, and fill it with hypertufa. When this has set, dig away the surrounding soil, heave the boulder out, and sculpt it with a chisel to reveal the top end of the copper pipe (cover this with a drilled pebble). Set up over a sump, so that the pump pushes water up the tube to dribble out over the boulder.

Step 5
Place an arrangement of cobblestones and pebbles around the boulders to cover the slabs and sump.

Step 4
Slide a drilled cobble over the end of the copper pipe, so the pipe is completely concealed.

Step 3
Use flexible pipe to link the pump to a length of copper pipe. Surround the copper pipe with boulders (or place a drilled boulder over it).

Variation using hypertufa

Single hypertufa boulder with drilled pebble in hollow

Step 1
Dig a hole and set the plastic sump in place complete with the sump lid and the pump.

Step 2
Lay a concrete slab over the sump to take the weight of the boulders.

The recipe for hypertufa is 1 part sand, 1 part cement, and 4 parts sphagnum moss. If you are planning a really big boulder, you will need lots of friends to help you heave it out of the hole.

HOW TO BUILD A MILLSTONE FOUNTAIN

A millstone fountain with a low, bell-shaped water spray—perfect for an exposed, windy position. Assorted cobblestones and gravel decorate the surrounding area.

← ↘ The working action of this feature is beautifully direct. The pump pushes water out of the fountain head that runs through the middle of the millstone. Water falls in a bell shape over the millstone and the surrounding pebbles, before finally seeping back into the sump. There are two real plus points with this project: the telescopic fountain head can be easily adjusted to suit the thickness of your millstone, and the tight bell shape of the falling water means that you don't have to fit an additional apron of plastic liner around the brim of the sump. If you are looking for a subtle, low-cost feature for an established area in the garden, which can be installed with the minimum of upheaval, this is the one to go for.

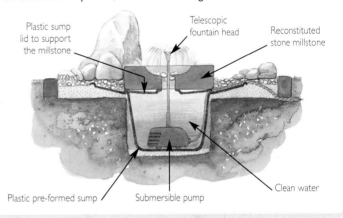

Plastic sump lid to support the millstone

Telescopic fountain head

Reconstituted stone millstone

Clean water

Plastic pre-formed sump

Submersible pump

MORE SELF-CONTAINED FOUNTAIN FEATURES

There are as many ideas for self-contained fountains as there are gardeners. If you are prepared to dig a bucket-size hole, and invest in a low-cost pump-and-sump installation, the possibilities are endless.

Fountains can be decorated with anything that won't be damaged by water, such as rocks, sculptures, glass bricks, shells, tiles, and cast-iron items.

Statuette fountain

↗ *A carefully chosen traditional statuette fountain is perfect for a small courtyard garden.*

Drilled cobblestone fountain

↗ *Water gently bubbling through a giant-size drilled feature cobblestone creates a cool, natural-looking spring.*

Japanese hewn stone fountain

↙ *The rough-hewn stone bowl and the everlasting flow of water suggest that this is a quiet, peaceful place to rest and meditate.*

Brimming pot fountain

↙ *The brimming pot is a symbol of good living, painting a picture reminiscent of free-flowing wine!*

Wall mask waterspouts

What is the best place for a wall mask waterspout?

If you have a small area that you want to set aside as a place for quiet contemplation—such as a courtyard patio, or a corner of the garden— consider installing a wall mask waterspout. This unobtrusive water feature will add to the atmosphere of your garden by contributing the relaxing sound of a gently trickling stream of water, sparkling as it falls into a pool below. It presents the opportunity to use an artistic mask to provide an additional focus of interest.

HOW TO BUILD A WALL MASK WATERSPOUT FEATURE

↘ → Study your site. Ideally, you need an existing garden wall in a sheltered corner away from draughts. If you do not have a suitable wall, look for an area where you can build a wall to head height. In either case, you will need the space to construct a reservoir at the base of the wall. Alternatively, existing containers can be used to provide a reservoir.

The waterspout consists of a pump placed in the reservoir, which is connected to a supply pipe that runs up the back of the wall and through into the mask.

EXISTING POND OR TANK

If you can use an existing cistern, sump, pool, trough, or old bathtub as the reservoir, to save you building this part of the project, so much the better. If you have a potential container, but it is unsightly, you could bury it in the ground.

Bricks and unusual tile inserts create a very decorative reservoir pool, complemented by a guard of plantpots.

Step 5
Bring the end of the supply pipe up the wall and through the mouth of the mask.

Step 3
Build a reservoir trough at the front of the wall. Render the inside with concrete and brush it with waterproof pond paint.

Step 2
Build a wall to about head height, with two holes for the supply pipe—at bottom center where it will connect to the pump, and toward the top of the wall where it will exit through the mask. If desired, insert a piece of slate into the front of the wall to break the water flow from the mask.

Step 4
Sit the pump in the reservoir, feeding the supply pipe and electricity supply through the lower hole in the wall.

Bricks

Try to design the project to use whole bricks rather than having to cut them. Do not attempt to tidy up the courses until the mortar is dry and crumbly (it feels sandy).

PUMP POWER

Measure the vertical distance between the surface of the water and the mouth of the mask (the head height). Add on 2 inches to allow for friction in the pipes and over-enthusiastic claims by the manufacturer, and then buy a low-voltage submersible pump to suit. Purchase the supply pipe to fit the pump. (See also pages 18–21.)

Step 1
Dig out the footing to a depth of 8 inches and lay a concrete slab to fill it.

COURTYARD GARDENS

If you are fortunate enough to have a courtyard garden complete with old walls, you need only to build the reservoir. If breaking up the adjacent paving is not an option, use a trough or cistern for the reservoir.

CONSIDER THE STYLE

If you don't want to use a mask, you can modify the design and use an item such as a spouting container, or a found object. For example, an antique faucet set over an old sink or bathtub would be a fun option, although unwary visitors might try to turn it off!

PROBLEMS WITH WALLS

Avoid using house walls: the ideal is a head-high garden wall. If you cannot run the pipe through the wall because of your neighbors, chisel out some of the mortar in the wall, then insert a narrow-gauge copper supply pipe and cover it with mortar or hanging tiles.

AN EASY-TO-BUILD WATERSPOUT

If your requirements are for a very straightforward project, which does not encroach on existing structures and can be finished in hours rather than days, try this simple solution.

You need a cistern or trough for the reservoir, a pump complete with plastic supply pipe, a mask made from ceramic or plastic resin, a wooden trellis, and a couple of potted climbing plants. Attach the trellis to an existing wall or a wooden frame. Place the reservoir in front of it and put the pump in the reservoir. Run the supply pipe from the pump, up behind the trellis, and through the mask. Cover the pipework with the climbers.

Wooden trellis and climbing plant

Wall mask

Supply pipe (connects submersible pump to wall mask)

Electricity supply

Decorative trough

OTHER WALL MASKS AND DESIGN VARIATIONS

Ancient mask

A pagan Green Man, with leafy fronds framing the head and snaking in at the mouth.

Animalistic mask

A lifesize lion's head, with a shaggy mane and a convincingly fearsome face.

Elemental mask

A figure to represent the wind. Sun, moon, and star masks are also available.

Classical mask

A Roman river god—an especially suitable character for a waterspout.

Breaking the water flow

→ If you want to create a more dramatic effect than a standard waterspout, with greater movement of water and more splashing, you can break the flow of the water by adding a basin. Some masks have an integral bowl and are intended as a complete feature, where a small pump is set directly in the bowl. However, you can set this unit over a larger reservoir, so the water spouts into the bowl and then splashes on into the reservoir. A tile mortared into the wall will create the same effect.

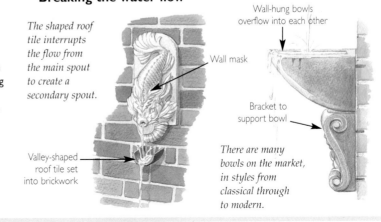

The shaped roof tile interrupts the flow from the main spout to create a secondary spout.

Wall mask

Valley-shaped roof tile set into brickwork

Wall-hung bowls overflow into each other

Bracket to support bowl

There are many bowls on the market, in styles from classical through to modern.

Japanese water features

Will a Japanese water feature suit my space?

There are quite a few water features of Japanese origin that will fit happily into Western gardens, whether or not they have a Japanese flavor. There is the simple water-filled stone basin or *chozubachi*; the *suikinkutsu*, which is a brimming stone basin with an underground echo chamber; and the more dramatic deer scarer or *shishi-odoshi*, where water trickles from a bamboo supply pipe into an upturned spout, creating a see-saw movement.

HOW TO BUILD A DEER SCARER

A deer scarer set up at the edge of a pond. The water is pumped out of the pond and up through the supply pipe.

↑ ↗ You need two pieces of bamboo: one piece 6 feet long and 2½ inches in diameter for the see-saw and supply pipe, and one piece 12 feet long and 4¾ inches in diameter for the two posts (all cut to different lengths). Water is pumped up from the pond and through the supply pipe, from where it trickles into the upturned end of the hollow bamboo see-saw. When the see-saw is full up, the balance is tipped and the water is poured back into the pond (which is acting as the sump). The end of the see-saw falls back on the striker stone with a heavy "clunk," and the sequence starts over again.

Step 2
Cut two support posts for the supply pipe, and the main post for the see-saw, from 4¾ inches bamboo. Sculpt the top of the support posts to a U-shape. Set the posts in the ground.

Step 3
Cut the supply pipe to length. Pierce the membranes in the supply pipe and the front end of the see-saw. Bridge the supply pipe across the support posts.

Step 4
Cut holes on opposite sides of the main post. Set the see-saw through the holes and pivot it in position with a whittled bamboo pin.

Step 5
Set the main post in the ground. Align the see-saw so that it is well positioned both to catch the water and shoot it back into the pond. Feed the PVC pipe into the supply pipe.

Striker stone

Step 1
Set the submersible pump in the pond, with the PVC pipe from the pump running underground to the inlet end of the supply pipe.

Alternative set-up using a sump
(for gardens without a pond)

→ Set a preformed plastic sump into the ground, complete with a pump, a generous amount of PVC water supply pipe, and an all-round liner apron to catch any water that splashes up. Set up the deer scarer as described, this time positioning the see-saw so that the water is shot on to a baffle stone, and then directed back into the sump.

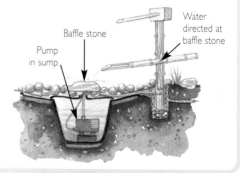

Baffle stone

Pump in sump

Water directed at baffle stone

VARIATIONS ON THE DEER SCARER

A directed head-on feed, where the supply pipe and see-saw are aligned at the empty, at-rest stage.

A more structured H-support and a block-and-pipe feed. There is a large striker stone at the rear.

The supply pipe and the see-saw share the same support—good for a pump-and-sump arrangement.

A minimal H-support and in-line supply pipe, plus a traditional brimming bowl feature made from hewn stone.

JAPANESE-STYLE WATER BASINS

Suikinkutsu stone
Basin with echo chamber

➜ The suikinkutsu stone echo chamber, or harp chamber, is uniquely beautiful in that it pleases both eye and ear. Water brims over the basin to drip down into a large pot set underground. The steady beat of the drip invites meditation.

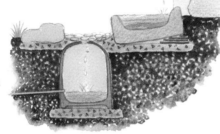

Tsukubai stone
Low basin

➜ Traditionally, the low, brimming tsukubai basin is designed to enhance a quiet, peaceful place where you might kneel or sit to meditate. Such bowls are usually set on a low stone platform or slab, with arrangements of special stones, shells, and plants all around.

Suiseki stone
Hypertufa basin

➜ The suiseki stone is defined as a natural basin, more of a found stone. The stone illustrated here is an interesting marriage of English and Japanese traditions, in that it is made from hypertufa, a mixture of cement, sand, and moss. It is easy to make, and visiting birds will love it.

WATER IN THE JAPANESE GARDEN

It is easy to give a Japanese flavor to a simple beam-and-plank bridge by adding a thick bamboo handrail and feature binding.

Water is an essential component of a traditional Japanese garden. Ponds, streams, pools, waterfalls, stepping stones, bridges, and basins all play a part in creating a certain environment.

In the West, we tend to want ponds and water features for reasons that are generally not voiced—for example, a pond is desirable because it is romantic. However, the Japanese have evolved a conscious, more structured way of thinking about garden features, which invests them with symbolism representing our physical and spiritual world. A stream symbolizes life force, a basin is a place for spiritual refreshment, a bridge is a place for making decisions, stones are mountains, raked grit is flowing water, stone lanterns light our path, and so on. To generalize, the Japanese build water features because they want to create shrines and places of meditation.

Rockery pools and rivulets

What sort of water feature could I put in a rockery?

Arockery is the ideal place to incorporate a rivulet together with a series of pools. A rivulet is a very small, fast-flowing stream. In a garden setting, a rivulet is often built as an addition to an established pond, creating a fast-moving miniature water feature. However, it is perfectly possible to build the feature in a rockery with no existing pond (or indeed to build a rockery from scratch), excavating pools and installing a pump as in previous projects.

HOW POOLS AND RIVULETS CAN BE BUILT INTO EXISTING ROCKERIES

(For a typical rockery, with a range of rocks set into a pile of soil.) Decide where the highest and lowest points are. Clear the rocks from these two areas and dig two shallow pools. The lower pool should be deep enough to take a small pump. Excavate a zigzag course from one pool to another. Set the pipes carrying the power and water supplies in place. Line the excavations with PVC, the higher areas overlapping the lower, so that water runs from one sheet of PVC to another. Cover the plastic with pebbles and gravel. Install the pump and fill the pools with water.

If the rockery in your garden is staid and rather uninspiring, a rivulet can add an exciting new dimension.

Points to consider

Scale ~ A rivulet needs to be kept small and fast-moving, and to follow a zigzag course. Could the slope be stepped to create rockpools?

Choice and placement of rocks ~ Look at your pond and consider how the rivulet can be shaped and guided along its route by a wall of selected rocks. Moss-covered rocks look good.

Plants ~ You need plants such as dwarf phlox (*Phlox subulata*) for the dry rockery, mosses for the damp rocks, and ferns, such as royal fern (*Osmunda regalis*) for the sides of the rivulet.

HOW TO BUILD A ROCKERY WITH POOLS AND A RIVULET

Step 2
Set the pipes in place. Roll the PVC liner over the top header pool and down the gully to lap into the lower reservoir pool.

Step 4
Plant the dry rockery and the sides of the damp gully with appropriate plants.

Step 1
Dig a hole for the preformed liner and set it in place. Use the excavated soil to sculpt the site.

Step 3
Fit the pump into the lower pool. Cover the liner with rocks, stones, and gravel, leaving pockets of soil for planting.

↗ → Decide on the site of the header and reservoir pools. Dig out the reservoir pool and fit a preformed liner. Use the spoil to grade the site so that a slight slope runs from the header pool to the reservoir. Sculpt the soil to create the rivulet gully. Dig in the water pipes. Roll a sheet of PVC liner from the header pool and down the gully, to lap into the reservoir pool. Fit the pump. Cover the liner with stones, cobblestones, gravel, and pockets of soil. Plant the site, fill the pools, and switch on the power.

Water flows down the slope and into a sump in the reservoir pool, where it is then pumped up to the header pool at the top of the slope to start over again.

Miniature water features

The best way of defining a miniature water feature is as a self-contained, pump-and-sump feature that is both portable and dynamic. It might be a tiny, solar-powered watermill set up on a sunny windowsill, or a do-it-yourself arrangement made from a couple of ceramic pots, a pump, and a collection of found stones. If it has circulating water, and is small enough to pick up in both hands, it can be described as a miniature water feature.

What is a miniature water feature?

DESIGNS FOR MINIATURE WATER FEATURES

A "seashore" fountain complete with beach finds—driftwood, shells, seaweed, and shingle.

A miniature millstone with a low bubbler fountain that lets water flow over the stone.

A bubbling fountain with a flow of water over a large, pre-drilled feature stone.

A barrel fountain: water brims over the top to run down from barrel to barrel.

HOW TO MAKE A MINIATURE POT FOUNTAIN

↘ You need two ceramic pots, a PVC liner, a small submersible pump with a telescopic fountain head jet, a flowerpot, a piece of wire netting, found items such as marbles, and some shingle. Water is pumped through the fountain head, where it spills on to the upper pot, overflows, and runs back down to the reservoir pot. When choosing the ceramic pots, remember that when the power is switched off, the bottom pot must be large enough to contain all the water.

Step 3
Lay a disk of wire netting to fit across the top of the reservoir pot just under the level of the pond liner.

Step 4
Sit the top pot in place and fill it with shingle topped with marbles. Spread shingle and marbles over the mesh in the reservoir pot.

Step 2
Fit the pump, complete with a wrap of masking tape around the extension tube (plug this through the flowerpot).

Step 5
Fill the bottom pot with water and switch on the power.

Step 1
Trim the PVC pond liner to fit the reservoir container, to end up just above the water line.

Step 6
Adjust the wrap of hole-blocking masking tape so that the top pot has chance to brim to overflowing.

The beautiful little fountain of water gradually fills the top pot to overflowing, so that the water runs over the collection of marbles and brass goldfish, and spills down the sides and back to the reservoir.

Sculptural water features

What makes a sculptural water feature?

Although water is part of the design of a sculptural water feature, the fact that it is a piece of sculpture is more important than its role as a water feature. The sculpture can be anything from a found stone that does no more than sit in water, as in the Japanese tradition, to a manufactured arrangement of metal and glass that holds water, or a series of items such as shells, with water running over the surface. There are many possibilities.

STARTING POINTS

Think about the places you enjoy going to and find stimulating. You might be inspired by the seashore, classical architecture, forest glades, or old industrial sites. Use this as a basis for recreating some of that atmosphere.

You could search out a large piece of weathered flat stone and just stand it in a shallow, shingle-covered pool, so that it looks like an ancient stepping stone—with the focus of the arrangement being the stone rather than the water. You could look for a piece of sculpture that is designed to hold water or to stand in water. You could sit a moss-covered tree root in a pool of water. A sculpture or found item is exciting in itself, but the aim is to display it so that part of its surface is in some way made more beautiful by being wet, lying in water, or being near water.

Sculpture for ponds

Sculptural water features are passive: water is present but it isn't pumped or thrown into motion in any way. If you like the idea of having a sculpture (found or made), and yet you want the water part of the design to be more dynamic, it would be better to opt for a traditional statuette fountain that uses a pump (see page 49).

NATURALISTIC DESIGNS

↗ *Inspired by both Japanese and Chinese traditions, the rain-catching or water-holding stone is a miniature waterscape. A single, carefully chosen stone can make a striking, shrinelike water feature and thought-provoking centerpiece.*

Naturalistic designs for sculptural water features fall into two categories: those composed almost entirely of natural found objects such as stones or a piece of a tree, and manufactured naturalistic representations of a figure, animal, or plant.

Manufactured items include cast metal sculptures, figures, large leaves, and suchlike, designed to be displayed at the water's edge. There are also geometrical items that have naturalistic forms as surface decoration. A good example of this is the traditional bird bath—a shallow bowl on a column, decorated with stylized imagery, perhaps with a statuette at its center.

← *A reconstituted stone bird bath, with stylized fern imagery on its surface and a little figure at its center.*

← *A small group of giant stones set in a minute pond—a perfect water feature for a small corner of a wild garden.*

ABSTRACT DESIGNS

Abstract designs don't seek to imitate nature. For example, a stone cube or sphere is abstract, while a carving in the shape of a leaf is naturalistic. However, some abstract designs, such as sculptures that are vaguely figurative in form, do draw inspiration from nature.

It is very difficult to say why some purely abstract forms excite our senses. Why, for example, is a stone cone sitting in a pool an inspirational form? The only way to proceed is to search out forms that you personally find exciting. If you see an item in a reclamation yard or a gallery, such as a stone disk or a cube, study its form and shape in relation to its potential as a water feature. Does it have a concave surface that will hold water? Does it have a texture that looks beautiful when wet? Consider such questions in relation to the style of your garden and the planned site for the sculpture.

Purely abstract sculptures
Sculptures inspired by geometry

↗ *This abstract design does feature moving water. It consists of a fountain head fixed to a copper pipe, surrounded by a tower of irregular stones stacked informally on an upside-down ceramic pot, which houses and protects the pump.*

↗ *A bird bath sculpture made from a lead tray with a display of old plumbing fittings. Perfect alongside a small pond.*

↗ *A single giant antique stone ball sitting in a shallow pool— an eye-catching detail for a large town garden.*

Figuratively abstract sculptures
Sculptures inspired by nature

↗ *A clam-shaped dish, with pebbles and shells. Good for a child's water play corner, or perhaps a bird bath.*

↗ *A sizeable stone sculpture inspired by a seed pod, with a bubbling fountain at its base. This striking feature would be suitable for a sophisticated, formal city garden.*

Sculpture and safety

Lifting large items of stone and metal, and setting sculptures in position, are potentially dangerous procedures. Take care when performing these tasks.

Structural strength ~ All sculptures, found and created, have an inherent structural integrity. Make sure that your chosen item is structurally fit for the intended purpose.

Footings ~ Big pieces of stone, metal, and wood must be set on a firm, concrete footing, especially if the intended site is near water.

Hazards ~ Is the sculpture so heavy or big that you will need help to set it in position? If it is to sit in water, will it harm the fish, discolor the water, or disintegrate? If it is polished stone, will the finish be damaged by the weather?

DIY creative water sculptures

How can I inject my own creativity into the garden?

If you want a really unique water feature in your garden, which will utilize your imaginative and creative abilities to the full, try a do-it-yourself water sculpture. It can be anything you want it to be. Perhaps you enjoy playing around with wood, metal, stone, or even old farm machinery. Many things can be employed to create an unusual sculpture that spins, whirls, twirls, swings, gushes, spouts, trickles, or whistles into motion, or just looks good in a watery situation.

The possibilities

The possibilities are endless: if you like a material or object, and it is safe and sound to use, go ahead and experiment.

Reclaimed machinery ~ Bits and pieces of old machinery, pumps, and fans, make wonderful kinetic sculptures.

Woodwork ~ Consider bamboo for Japanese water sculptures, logs for bridges, or perhaps carved wooden figures.

Metalwork ~ Sheet metal, copper, and brass can be cut and beaten into shape. Good for containers, bowls, and figures.

Stonework ~ Stone can be cut with a chisel or assembled. Look at Japanese lanterns, figures, bird baths, balls, and cones.

Concrete work ~ Concrete can be cast, sculpted, troweled and textured into sinks, urns, bowls, figures, slabs, abstract forms, Japanese lanterns, wall masks, balls, cones, and fountains.

A swirling mass of old chains, encircled by a low box hedge, creates a stunning form that has been turned into a dynamic water feature.

CASCADING WATER SCULPTURES

In the copper cascade sculpture shown on the right, water is pumped up to the top of the railroad ties and out of a spout to cascade down a series of copper cups, eventually seeping back to the pond to start over again. The cups are made from folded copper sheet, but other items such as metal bowls, bits salvaged from old machinery, old watering cans, or discarded teapots may also be suitable.

↘ *This cascade sculpture draws water from a pond. However, it could also be positioned over a sump or next to a trough.*

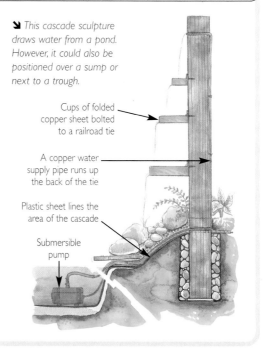

Cups of folded copper sheet bolted to a railroad tie

A copper water supply pipe runs up the back of the tie

Plastic sheet lines the area of the cascade

Submersible pump

↗ *Copper is an attractive and versatile material—this series of copper cups welded to copper pipe is arranged to make a striking double cascade.*

↗ *A contemporary design, featuring geometric shapes, for a wall-mounted copper sculpture positioned over a raised pool that acts as a reservoir.*

"WHO'S-LEFT-THE-WATER-ON?" SCULPTURE

There are many variations on the "who's-left-the-water-on?" theme, some with pumps and others with faucets. This particular sculpture is a faucet mounted on top of a post. Water is pumped directly from the sump up to the faucet, whereupon it falls back into the sump, giving the illusion that the faucet has been left on. The set-up is so convincing that strangers may try to turn the faucet off. An old chrome faucet purchased from a yard sale has been used, but you could use anything from a brass faucet to an iron water pump. Make sure that you remove the washer mechanism, so that the faucet cannot be turned off.

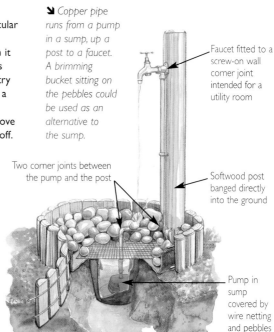

↘ *Copper pipe runs from a pump in a sump, up a post to a faucet. A brimming bucket sitting on the pebbles could be used as an alternative to the sump.*

Faucet fitted to a screw-on wall corner joint intended for a utility room

Two corner joints between the pump and the post

Softwood post banged directly into the ground

Pump in sump covered by wire netting and pebbles

← *A variation on the theme—an iron pump set over a half-barrel that acts as the sump. This sculpture also requires an old iron hand pump, a small electric pump, and a length of PVC tube.*

WATER-PROPELLED SCULPTURE

There are many types of water-propelled sculpture—everything from those inspired by a ship's screw propeller or a watermill, to those that resemble a child's windmill. If you are interested in the idea of a water-propelled sculpture, but cannot settle on a design, it is a good idea to experiment.

Take a circle of aluminum foil and use scissors to cut a gradual spiral to its center. Hang this from a cotton thread and dangle it under a running faucet to see how it spins. Repeat the experiment with a child's windmill. Continue experimenting by making lots of aluminum foil and card prototypes before you start working with copper sheet, sumps, and pumps.

↗ *A spiral cut from flat copper sheet hangs from a length of fishing line and spins under the flow of water.*

↗ *A copper wheel (just like a child's windmill, but cut from flat sheet) spins under the flow of water.*

OTHER WATER-PROPELLED WATER FEATURES

There are two ways that flowing water can be employed to run a sculpture. It can be used (like the wind) to set a pivoted wheel spinning, or it can be used as a weight to operate a lever, so that water flows from one pivoted container to another, just like a Japanese deer scarer.

If you are good with a soldering iron, you could use thin sheet metal such as lead or copper. If you enjoy woodwork, you could build models or work with bamboo. If you like playing around with found items, you could adapt a child's windmill or experiment with containers such as plastic bowls or metal pots. We have seen a sculpture made from three metal teapots—the pump topped up one teapot to the point where it tipped on a pivot and transferred its water to the second teapot, and so on down the line. There are many exciting options. Whatever your idea, it is important to make prototypes and experiment with them under water flowing from a faucet.

Index